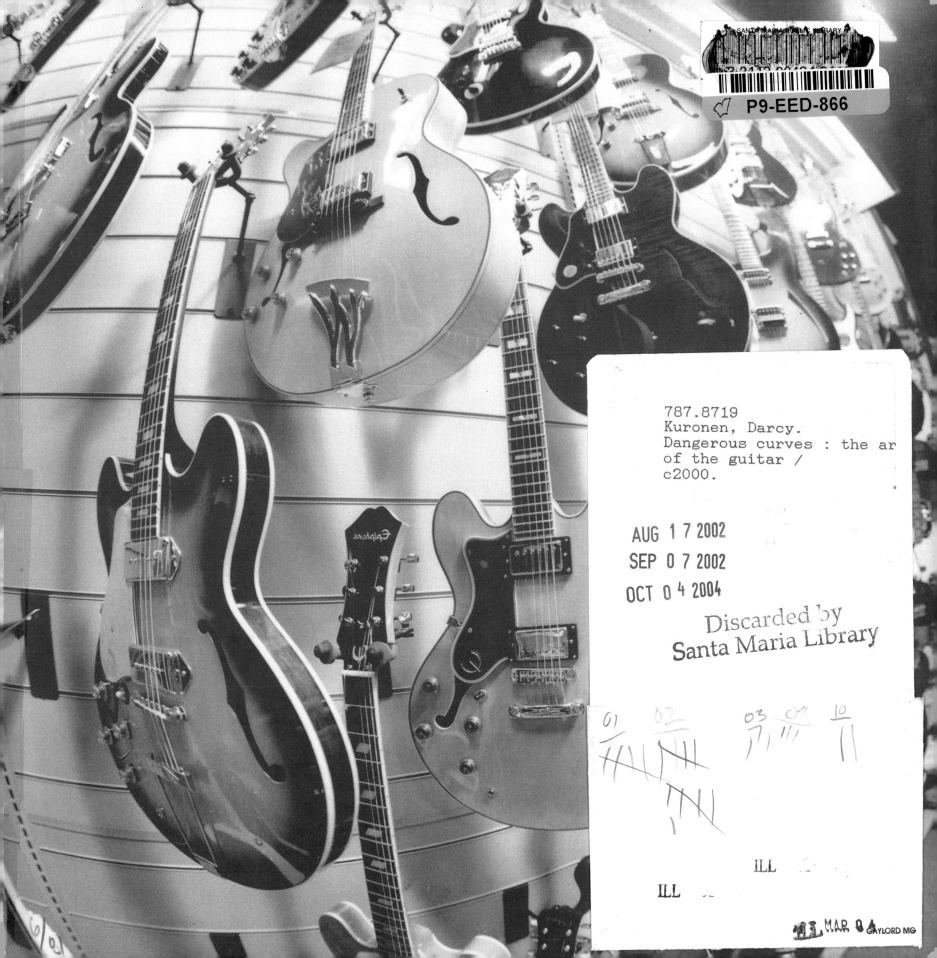

DANGEROUS CURVES
THE ART OF THE GUITAR

Darcy Kuronen

Foreword by Lenny Kaye
Photographs by Carl Tremblay
and others

MFA PUBLICATIONS
a division of the Museum of Fine Arts, Boston

MFA Publications
a division of the Museum of Fine Arts, Boston
295 Huntington Avenue
Boston, Massachusetts 02115

Published in conjunction with the exhibition "Dangerous Curves: Art of the Guitar," organized by the Museum of Fine Arts, Boston, from November 5, 2000, to February 25, 2001.

ISBN 0-87846-478-6 cloth
ISBN 0-87846-485-9 paper
Library of Congress Catalog Card Number: 99-069929

The publishers express their gratitude to the editors of *Guitar Player* for their kind permission to reproduce guitarists' statements that originally appeared in the magazine's pages, with the following exceptions:

pp. 26, 30, 54, 72 (courtesy Folklore Productions), 91 (courtesy Leo Kottke), 92 (courtesy David Bromberg), 100 (courtesy Becky Byrd and Lindy S. Martin Personal Management), 158, 166 (courtesy Ani DiFranco and Righteous Babe Records), 181 (courtesy David Bromberg), and 216.

Excerpt on page 150 from "Perfectly Good Guitar," written by John Hiatt. © 1993 Careers-BMG Music Publishing, Inc. (BMI). All rights reserved. Used by permission.

Endpaper photograph taken at Mars, The Musician's Planet
Hand on page 8 modeled by Reeves Gabrels

Designed by Ed Marquand, Marquand Books, Inc., Seattle, Washington
www.marquand.com
Printed and bound at CS Graphics Pte., Ltd., Singapore

Available through D.A.P./Distributed Art Publishers
155 Sixth Avenue, 2nd floor
New York, New York 10013
Tel. (212) 627-1999 · Fax (212) 627-9484

First edition
Printed in Singapore

CONTENTS

DIRECTOR'S STATEMENT

OF THE MANY WONDERFUL AND DIVERSE OBJECTS in the Museum of Fine Arts, Boston, musical instruments offer special fascination for visitors. They have the ability to transport us back in time and to distant places, whether a harpsichord suited to the preludes of Bach or a sitar that evokes an Indian raga. We are likewise drawn to their graceful forms, beautifully wrought designs that not only are aesthetically pleasing but also serve the acoustic and ergonomic needs of the player—a remarkable marriage of form and function.

Musical instruments have seldom formed the subject of a major museum exhibition, and perhaps never before one that explores them primarily from a visual perspective. If any instrument lends itself to this treatment it is the guitar. Its sensuous contours have inspired manifold interpretations, from the petite, slim-bodied form used for the earliest examples to the generously proportioned "jumbo" and "dreadnought" models of the twentieth century. But while many guitar makers have lavished their efforts on instruments with the traditional waisted shape, others have consistently tried other outlines and designs that often encroach on the realm of sculpture and decorative art.

Among the many roles assumed by art museums is an effort to challenge the way we look at the world around us—to raise awareness of good design and examine how tastes in the styling of material objects is constantly changing. The four-hundred-year history of the guitar offers a particularly engaging approach. *Dangerous Curves: The Art of the Guitar* presents a unique look at one of the most recognizable, yet most varied, images of our culture.

— MALCOLM ROGERS
Ann and Graham Gund Director of the Museum of Fine Arts, Boston

ACKNOWLEDGMENTS

THIS BOOK AND ITS ACCOMPANYING EXHIBITION would not have been possible without the help of a number of people, all of whom enthusiastically supplied assistance in a variety of ways. I would like to particularly express my gratitude to the following colleagues, who were exceptionally generous in their support and guidance: Tony Bingham, James Bollman, Richard Bruné, Walter Carter, Scott Chinery, Brian Fischer, Stan Werbin, and Michael Wright.

I would also like to thank the many other private collectors, scholars, performers, guitar makers, and personnel at museums who graciously gave of their time and advice: Scot Michael Arch, Chet Atkins, Tony Bacon, Howard Bass (Smithsonian Institution), Charles Beare (J. & A. Beare, Ltd.), Perry Beekman, Carmelle Bégin (Museé des Civilisations), Peter Blecha (Experience Music Project), Dick Boak (Martin Guitars), Del Breckenfeld (Fender Guitars), David Bromberg, Kix Brooks, Ken Butler, Doug Chandler (PRS Guitars), Emmett Chapman (Stick Enterprises), Dennis Cinelli, Brian Cohen, Brenda Colladay (Gaylord Entertainment), Jol Dantzig (Hamer USA), Frédéric Dassas (Musée de la Musique), Andrew Dipper (Claire Givens Violins), Joël Dugot (Musée de la Musique), Ben Elder, Steve Evans (Jacksonville Guitars), Larry Fishman (Parker Guitars), Frank Ford (Gryphon Stringed Instruments), Jim Forderer, Charles Fox, Scott Frelich (Top Shelf Music), Laela French (Autry Museum of Western Heritage), Reeves Gabrels, J. Geils, Rick Gembar (Gibson Musical Instruments), Roy Goode, Al Greenwood (*Vintage Guitar Magazine*), George Gruhn (Gruhn Guitars, Inc.), John Hall (Rickenbacker International Corp.), Olav Chris Henriksen, Michael Holmes, Tom Van Hoose, Steve Howe, Dee Hoyt, Don Johnson (Ovation Instruments), Richard Johnston (Gryphon String Instruments), Kerry Keane, Stacey Kluck (Smithsonian Institution), Frank Koonce, John Koster (America's Shrine to Music Museum), Randall Kremer, Tim Kummer (Mars, The Musician's Planet), André P. Larson (America's Shrine to Music Museum), Laurence Libin (Metropolitan Museum of Art), Darryl Martin (Edinburgh University), Mike McGuire (Gibson Musical Instruments), J. Kenneth Moore (Metropolitan Museum of Art), Jim Mouradian, Vincent Motel, Arnold Myers (Edinburgh University), Rick Nielsen, Randy

Osborne (Fine Fretted String Instruments), Fred Oster (Vintage Instruments), John Page (Fender Museum of the Arts Foundation), Ken Parker (Parker Guitars), Les Paul, Joseph Peknik (Metropolitan Museum of Art), Ronald Perera (Smith College Music Department), Stewart Pollens (Metropolitan Museum of Art), Alison Poulson (Autry Museum of Western Heritage), Richard Rephann (Yale University), Tim Scheerhorn, Greg Skavhaug, Paul Reed Smith (PRS Guitars), Richard R. Smith, Jim Speros, Walter Stanul, Gary Sturm (Smithsonian Institution), David A. Stutzman (Stutzman's Guitar Center), Alex Timmerman, Alex Usher, John Vanco (Erie Art Museum), Mike Voltz (Gibson Musical Instruments), Frank Wallace, Lon Werner (Martin Guitars), Tim White, and Mac Yasuda.

Malcolm Rogers, Ann and Graham Gund Director, and Kathryn Getchell, Deputy Director for Curatorial Administration, have been extremely supportive of this project since its inception, and I must also thank Brent Benjamin, former Deputy Director for Curatorial Affairs, for discussions that led to the idea of a guitar exhibition at the Museum. A dedicated staff working in the Museum's Department of Musical Instruments assisted in a myriad of details involved in borrowing and researching such a large number of guitars; my sincere thanks to Abaigeal Duda, Stephanie Morse, and Andrew Scott. I would also like to thank Pat Loiko, Registrar, for ably arranging transport of all the instruments to Boston, and Mark Polizzotti, Publisher, for his encouragement and supervision throughout the preparation of this book. Many other colleagues at the Museum must also be acknowledged for their contributions to the success of this undertaking, including Ellenor Alcorn, Paul Bessire, Jennifer Bose, Tanya Contos, Dawn Griffin, John Hermann, Peter Littlefield, Tom Lang, Peter der Manuelian, Anne L. Poulet, D. Samuel Quigley, Joellen Secondo, David Strauss, and Gerald W. R. Ward. I was also very pleased to work with Carl Tremblay and his assistant Rod Mclean, who produced the book's beautiful photographs, and with Ed Marquand, who oversaw the wonderful design.

Finally, heartfelt thanks to my wife, Melissa, and my son, Niles, for listening to me talk about nothing but guitars for the past two years.

— DK, MARCH 2000

PREFACE

FROM COURT MUSICIANS serenading sixteenth-century royalty to rock bands blasting megawatts in packed stadiums, the guitar has been an enduring musical icon for over four centuries. To a far greater degree than any other instrument, it has been interpreted with extraordinary variety of form and decoration, always reflecting the aesthetics of the time. This is as true for ornate guitars of the Baroque era, inlaid with ivory and pearl, as it is for twentieth-century electric instruments painted in blue metallic flake. *Dangerous Curves: The Art of the Guitar* celebrates this diversity, displaying how changes in fashion, technology, and musical tastes have influenced the look of the world's most popular instrument.

The gratifying sound that even novice players can obtain from the guitar has always been one of its most attractive qualities. Likewise, its portability and capacity to produce chords, melody, and bass have made it an ideal instrument for impromptu music making. For purists, there is none but the classical guitar, which struggled for and eventually won acceptability in the realm of art music. But the guitar has taken on so many other musical roles, especially in the twentieth century. The fancy and expensive instruments made for cowboy singing stars and jazz musicians of the 1930s and 1940s were conspicuous reflections of their owners' image and success. Among folk singers, plainer-looking guitars became emblems of social protest. And to countless youths, the sheer volume produced by the electric guitar has made it a powerful means of rebellion and self-expression.

Of the many purposes the guitar has served over the centuries, it has perhaps excelled most as a tool of seduction. Although often depicted in the hands of gentlewomen in earlier centuries, it has more often been the lady herself who has fallen under the spell of a fellow who could strum even a few simple chords. Commentators have also long observed the similarity of the guitar's curvaceous shape to that of a woman, as well as the suggestive way the player (usually male) cradles its body and strokes its strings, the vibrations intimately transmitted to his own chest. Conversely, the aggressive performance style of many electric guitarists has led others to analyze the instrument as a phallic symbol or weapon. Either way, there is something fascinating about physical interaction with the guitar. The piano is operated like a machine and drums are often beaten like an opponent, but the guitar is embraced in the arms and worn like a talisman.

It is specifically because the guitar has avoided strict association with classical music and the concert hall that luthiers have been free to adopt such a wide variety of shapes and decorative schemes for the instrument's construction. Makers of acoustic models have experimented since the beginning with every variation of size and proportion to the waisted form, and have at times dispensed with it altogether. But with the advent of the solid-body electric guitar in the mid-twentieth century, designers became truly free to impose nearly any shape, color, and texture on the instruments they created. The typically rounded shapes of the guitar sometimes gave way to dramatically angular ones, and sometimes yielded design "innovations" that had actually been developed centuries before. The maker may believe an idea is unique and new, but given the long and diverse history of the guitar, completely original concepts are increasingly rare.

Selecting the guitars for this book was understandably subjective, but also, given the tremendous number of interesting and beautiful instruments from which to choose, extremely challenging. The aim was to strike a balance between models that have been especially successful or influential, examples that attempted to redefine what a guitar can be, and instruments that have a particularly interesting story behind their design. Aficionados may find inexplicable absences, but readers will also surely discover many musical treasures among these delightful, amazing dangerous curves.

FOREWORD

BY LENNY KAYE

THE VIBRATING STRING. The sound wave in motion, one of the most primitive means of measuring pitch. The vocal cord made manifest.

The guitar is the preeminent instrument of the twentieth century, with a tail winding deep into the fossil record of musical millennia past, and a head-stock looking curiously into the next hundred-year span. Museum enshrining—such as the exhibit at Boston's Museum of Fine Arts that prompted this book—implies an exaltation of where we've been. What better moment to bear witness to the splendor of the guitar as it continually relocates the music it will become?

I'm no innocent bystander. I play the guitar, not an unusual calling in these times when most everybody knows a couple of chords, or knows somebody who does. The guitar is the parlor instrument of the past hundred years, replacing the piano in the living room and the neighborhood bar. It's about as simple as can be, and you can sing along. Or you can devote a lifetime to unraveling its intricacies. Something for everybody.

It's a physical instrument, touch-sensitive, and responds equally well to gently caressing soft minor diminisheds in the moonlight, or being hacked against the frame of an amplifier hanging by a sway bar (see also whammy bar, wang bar, or tailpiece vibrato).

It's portable. You can carry it anywhere (slung over one's shoulder in an old pillowcase is the accepted mode of transport in my neighborhood), and with the addition of even the smallest electronic gain booster, preferably soaked in tubes, it can be heard for miles around.

You can play any kind of music on it. It lends itself equally well to the polyphonic classics as it does to basic chord-and-a-half rock, jazzbo comping, and country fried chicken-pickin'; and once electrified, it has a tonal palette unrivaled in expressiveness, that is, if you like fuzz tone, reverb, flanging, and tremolo. Clean or dirty. Mid-boost. Master volume.

As the guitar flowed west from Europe—with a nudge from Africa and Asia—over the course of centuries to find lodging in the El Dorado that is

13

America, the home of Messrs. Rickenbacher, Martin, Gibson, and the sainted Leo Fender (and Les Paul, the fulcrum upon which all these hollow- and solid-body visionaries balanced their evolutionary pickup ideas), it became nigh ubiquitous. Now, with the final chord feedbacking on the century—one that began with a people's instrument sold in the Sears, Roebuck catalog for five dollars and ended with the infinite possibilities of digital encoding—it's time to tune up.

There is something fundamentally bass-ackwards about a museum exhibition of guitars. When instruments are removed from their function—i.e., sounding—we are constrained merely to look at objects that were meant to be heard. We can only imagine their tone, their sustain, the sound bouncing around the interior of a hollowed-out body or projected through magnetized poles into the electronic airstream. Aloud: that is how a guitar is meant to be perceived.

And then there is touch. I can tell you that hardly anything feels more silky than the neck of a '57 Stratocaster, its varnish worn away by countless barre chords, the slight hollow where the palm cups the higher notes. It positively glows with the warm fibers of its wood, its striations and grains breathing. Read it geologically, like a rock formation worn by the wind, revealing strata, upheavals, sudden aftershocks, and the continual wear-and-tear of centuries.

Guitars impart the personality of their players' skills, the nicks and scars of their playing. Pete Townshend's smashed SG, the pick marks scraped along the guard. Chet Atkins's courteous, restrained Country Gentleman, which responds more to the filigree than to the flamboyance. Jimi Hendrix's upside-down Strat. B. B. King's Lucille. Truly, these are instruments meant to be held, if only in the imaginary music they make as they wait in readiness, the promise of melody and rhythm awaiting their performer.

For those guitars whose owners aren't well known, or whose owners never play them, the visual appeal is still visceral. We slide slowly into matters of style here, not only musical genre but popular geometry, the arrangement of shapes and sizings and decorative touches that spotlight our given instant of culture. The hourglass figure, the quality of varnish, the inlay all capture the moment of the instrument's intersection with the newsreel; the scratch of a 78 record, the saturated Cinerama colors of a 1950s Bible movie, the dark gleam of a 1930s Gibson gamboled down a Mississippi crossroads at midnight, making its deal with the devil.

Shape is fluid, within the reasonable bounds of what a guitar basically is. Start from the premise that you need a board on which to stretch the strings, a means to tune them and project them, only two hands (at the outer limits of which you invent the pedal steel, but they—musician and instrument—are a breed apart). The basic blueprint of the guitar is established. From there, it becomes a matter of custom shopping.

A neck. Staggered frets, crosswise across the length to specify intonation, or fretless, like a violin, its nearest relation in the string-along clan. Any number of strings, really, though most guitars have half a dozen; the twelve-string a high-strung half-brother. Mario Maccaferri had a nine-string; Korn favors the seven-string. Tuning is a myriad of secret handshakes, but usually it's chord-based, all the better to bend with a minimum of fingers, preparing to plant the rest in a nearby seventh.

You don't choose a guitar; it chooses you, and shapes your playing—form follows function follows fashion. The music's silhouette is delineated and then customized by each player, involving and evolving. The birth of the blues. Rock and roll. Don't forget to wiggle it around, just a little bit; Jerry Lee Lewis made his entire eighty-eight-stringed instrument sound like a guitar in "Whole Lotta Shakin' Goin' On." And from the same '50s Sun studio, Scotty Moore gave the new music a swimming, echo echo repeats per second. The guitar made way for entire subculted languages, created its own ultrasound image, much as the well-tempered clavier assisted Bach in his watch-like contrapuntal precision, or the smeared and pedaled piano allowed Debussy his liquid sense of dappled light and dark, his pedal steel.

When someone asks me what kind of guitar to buy, I say the one that makes you want to pick it up. That you'll leave lying across the bed, on a chair, within easy reach. The one you'll keep playing. Plumage is important. The haze of a color, the adornment, the artisanship all play their part in a guitar's costuming, its character, its role. A decade or two down the line, the guitar that you bought new in a music store hanging on a rack with a dozen others (all of which were quite beguiling, thank you) will have opened up its resonance, stretched its wood in appreciation of the music that has been made, and accommodated all willing hands, or just yours and yours alone. An instrument requires respect, give and take. You should get to know each other.

The guitar is a family member, of the family Chordophone, and the following assemblage is a rare reunion. I can imagine the instruments in the Boston MFA exhibition climbing down from their displays after hours, gathering for a late-night shoot of the breeze, seeing what distant cousins have been up to, intermingling their musics. And because families help each other out, one will gift a lick to a relation struggling in some new clime, and a new music might get born. You never know.

The guitar is a strummer's instrument: a strolling harp, the perfect tool for a wandering minstrel. In the heyday of the Renaissance lute, guitars began to mutate. By 1300, there existed a *guitarra moresca*, which resembled a lute, and a *guitarra latina*, a primitive antecedent more closely emphasizing the cinched waist and boned corset of the guitar torso. They'd met in Spain. You can see how intermarriage would produce such an offspring.

For a while, the guitar was the prodigal, tumbling down the slippery slopes of class until it found root in the non-courtly orders. The curvature of its upper and lower bouts gave it a disconcerting sensuality that removed it from polite society. Life in back alleys and taverns simplified the instrument to its bare essentials, refined its basic uses. In the early 1600s, the *chitarra* was widespread enough to warrant Italian instruction books. Working its way back to the drawing room and concert stage during the 1800s, leaving the *duende—* the spirit-elf—of flamenco in its wake, the guitar stayed underfoot (better for dancing) in the roadhouses and the hills, until the folk boom of the 1960s. With the guitar-slingers of rock and roll, it became a social signifier, not only an instrument but an accepted lifestyle accessory and symbol of personal liberation. Once only a player in the orchestra, now it stepped out to lead the band. Took a spotlight solo. Made it big time.

That's the short view. The long unfolds in the overlapping concentric orbits of each instrument's role as a go-between in the tacit trio that is player and music and listener.

We have turned up the volume on the electric century. If there is a narrative to accompany this procession of stringed instruments, it is the guitar's journey to its amplification, its desire to be heard, and the musics created in its wake.

The guitar is the only major instrument to be so transformed by a wall outlet and a pronged plug. It perches on the borderline separating sound generated from within and the ventriloquism projected through an out-of-body source, manipulating its character.

The enhancement of acoustics began early in the 1920s and resulted in such wonders as the microphone, radio, and talkies. It would change the way singers sing and actors act. Les Paul remembers sitting in his Waukesha, Wisconsin, living room wondering how these relatively new technologies might be combined, jamming a phonograph record needle into the wood of his guitar and sending it through the wire-coiled magnet of a telephone mouthpiece into a radio speaker in hopes of generating an electron stream that might be embellished in amplitude and tone. Literally sculpting air.

Early luthiers understood the vibration of the woods they filed and carved into shape. Each guitar was like an ecology, each piece harmonic. With a minimum of moving parts, the instrument was a tinkerer's dream, and even the simplest innovation could radically transform its sound and attack. When Christian Frederick Martin brought his art and craft from the Viennese workshop of Johann Staufer to America in 1833, he braced the soundboard of his instruments in the shape of an X. Thus strengthened, the guitar would eventually be able to accommodate the grander overtone tensionings of steel strings, instead of the gut or silver wire over silk that ran through the courses of European instruments. The ringing appealed to the industrial clamor of the new twentieth century.

Orville Gibson also liked the clang of steel. He thought the guitar came up short compared with the sophistication of the violin. Working in a music store in Kalamazoo, Michigan, he combined what he felt were the violin's best design qualities into his mandolins, zithers, and harp guitars, arching the top of the instruments and eventually selling his patents to a consortium of investors in the early 1900s who took his designs to the mass guitar market.

Gibson's arch vs. Martin's flat-top. The note swirled around the belly of one, spun like a centrifuge from the circulatory soundhole of the other, neck and inlaid neck through the first third of the century. The tone shapes within the outer shell of the instrument, molding a frequency of interior space, pumped through the body's soundhole—or in 1923, the arch top's scrolled f-holes—to awaiting ears. Now Eddie Lang didn't have to keep time on the banjo, and could chop and dice his comps on the big Gibson L-5; Martin's Dreadnought series would become a bluegrass standard. Not all sounds are burnished in the instrument's rib cage: there is the scrape of the pick striking the strings, the thump of the forearm as it hugs the guitar body, the hissing snake of the hip, and the ever-tapping foot.

With the mirror-image twin streams of country blues—Charley Patton, Willie McTell, Robert Johnson—and country string bands—Carter Family, Fields Ward and His Mountaineers, Gid Tanner and His Skillet Lickers—coming to prominence in the 1920s and 1930s, both driven by the guitar's sidekick accompaniment, and the blue yodeling figure of Jimmie Rodgers perhaps straddling both, the instrument was well positioned to attack the flanks of the hit parade. But in the swing era, only western combos allowed the guitar a prominence; back East, where horns ruled the urban bandstand, the guitar's role was still essentially rhythmic. The great Gypsy guitarist Django Reinhardt brought a dapper flair to the instrument, perhaps one of the first crossovers plying a folk

17

tradition into a more sophisticated Hot Club musicality (though even there, jazz was a little suspect). Along with Charlie Christian—who had just gotten one of the first amplifiers to trade solo fours with Benny Goodman's orchestra—Les Paul, Alvino Rey, and Merle Travis helped extend the instrument's wingspan through World War II, by which time Muddy Waters, Arthur "Guitar Boogie" Smith, Paul Burlison, and Link Wray were ready to plug in.

When Bobby "Bill Parsons" Bare told the story of an "All-American Boy" in 1959—"Get yourself a gui-tar / Put it in tune / You'll be a-rockin' and a-rollin' soon"—he was heralding an explosion in the instrument's popularity. Funky chicken or cracked egg, the guitar launched the instant gratification of rock and roll, along with the magnetic attraction of a solid-body pulsing with its own electrocuting song, the hum and buzz of an axe turned up to Spinal Tap's "11."

When does a guitar become something else? When is it not a guitar? Electricity opened a philosophical debate that, regardless of which side you argued, inflamed passions to a seismic degree and drew a fault line that could have collapsed in on itself or changed the role of the instrument forever.

The guitar was lucky. Unlike the harpsichord making way for the pianoforte (and what about the mellotron, not to mention synthesizers?), its playing heritage—tunings, number of strings, and vast literature, from Fernando Sor to countless Appalachian ballads—meant the difference was more tonal and attitudinal. Guitars could continue to do what they did best: proliferate, evolve.

The rush to electricity expanded the playing field, broadening the guitar's horizons, making it nigh indispensable. No longer confined to a subliminal supporting role within a band's momentum, it could be the undeniable focal point. But when the time came for the formal introduction of electricity, the source was unlikely: a small chain of archipelagoes as distant from the United States as America is wide, Hawaii.

The acoustic lap steel is played with a bar in the neck hand, resting flat, and in the 1920s became a popular recording instrument via the island stylings of such as Frank Ferara and Sol Hoopii. Its wiry tone and melodic phrasing, with many slurs and vibratos, lent well to the acoustic horns that would capture sound before 1925, the year Bell Laboratories introduced their electrical recording process. The image of hula maidens and beachfront sunsets didn't hurt. I am reminded of this gazing at the National Triolian in my corner, waiting for me to tickle its strings, which stretch over a conical diaphragm resonator, a virtual speaker in a completely metal guitar, painted bronze, with a palm tree stenciled on the back. Those were adventurous times.

Ironically, the acoustic lap steel—tied as it was to an island vogue—faded as electrical recording became the norm. But Adolph Rickenbacher had a manufacturing outlet that pressed National's steel bodies, and so came in contact with George Beauchamp, who had partnered John Dopyera at National and helped pioneer the resonator guitar. Beauchamp was still working on how to make the guitar louder when a disagreement with Dopyera moved him into partnership with Rickenbacher. Both saw a niche where they could apply George's ideas of doing away with the soundhole altogether. Out of the Frying Pan (his most famous creation, driven by a pair of horseshoe-shaped magnets) and into the fire. Once amplifiers were onstage, it was a simple matter to adapt them to guitars, and the guitars themselves began to transform.

Suddenly, the body of the guitar could look like anything. Practicality and comfort considerations led to a semistandardized sense of how an electric guitar should appear, give or take a single or double cutaway, but Bo Diddley could play a square box, for all it mattered, and Valco (themselves big in the lap steel business, witness the mother-of-pearloid Supro) could make their Brentwood in the shape of the U.S. of A. In fiberglass, no less.

The populuxe styling of the '50s replicated the Detroit tail fin and sense of roar that was America in midcentury. Leo Fender, in a southern California that was a custom car hotspot and future surfing Mecca, invented the Broadcaster in 1948, improving on it with the Telecaster and then the Stratocaster (the Jag-Stang would come much later), a template of American archetypes that now constitutes one of the great guitar lineages and has the surf music to prove it.

Gibson saw its arch top demand fall off sharply after World War II. Though it matched Martin model for model in the flat-top acoustic field (Martin opted for the traditional—they never successfully went electric, though Bob Dylan certainly did), Gibson had promoted "electrical" arch-top guitars as early as 1936. Charlie Christian used an ES 150, and the bar pickup it featured is now nicknamed for him. Yet when Les Paul brought a homemade solid-body electric to Gibson in 1941, a pine plank on which he'd affixed two pickups and a bridge, surrounding it with pieces from an Epiphone guitar body to make it look less alien, they referred to it as a broomstick and passed.

The company could hardly ignore the stir that Fender was creating. Already the Telecaster was influencing guitar phrasings; the bright, brittle sound could cut through drums and bass and the most unruly audiences. So in alliance with Les Paul, who by now had graduated to his own garage studio and the wonders of multitracking, Gibson designed a guitar with low-end authority and endless sustain, a slightly carved top to recall its violinistic inspirations, and gold finish, because "what other color?" It became the Les Paul in 1952 (make mine '59 and tiger-striped), and remains a fitting namesake for a man who was in the forefront of guitar invention. Regardless of which one reached the Pole first, "The Log" is arguably the first pure electric guitar.

Adolph Rickenbacker (he'd hardened his name's spelling along the way) was not about to miss out on this frontier opened up for settlement. Even after he retired in the 1940s, his company continued their off-the-beaten-path explorations. They were a favorite with the new English bands, especially the Beatles' John Lennon, and they had a unique item with their electric twelve-string guitar, which would be anointed the mediator between folk and rock in the hands of Roger McGuinn of the Byrds, a band consciously formed as a link between the Beatles and Dylan.

The '60s sparked the fuse to a guitar boom. A host of manufacturers rushed in to answer the skyrocketing demand. Some, like Epiphone and Kay, were older firms modernizing; others, like Guild or the later Mosrite (endorsed by the Ventures, an all-guitar band that taught many young guitarists their opening licks), adapted themselves to the times. Soon the sound of a painstakingly formed E chord was echoing from garages across the land.

Luthiers became modern assembly-line factories, churning out literally millions of guitars. Though the sheer numbers gave the instrument a workaday, journeyman quality, it didn't necessarily mean any less emphasis on personality. If anything, guitar makers seemed only too anxious to indulge their most extravagant fantasies. Gibson flipped out and produced the Flying V and Explorer. Gretsch had been manufacturing guitars in Brooklyn since the 1930s, but their association with Chet Atkins in 1955 prompted a Nashville swivel for the company. They soon had the Tennessean and the Country Club models, though Gretsch's zenith would be reached with the exquisite White Falcon (we won't even mention the impossibly rare White Penguin), a six-stringed metal-flaked spangle of c&w fashion. There were individual high-end artisans crystallizing tradition, the exquisite arch tops of D'Angelico and D'Aquisto; and budget lines, with everybody's first guitar, a Silvertone built by the Danelectro company of Neptune, New Jersey, amp in the guitar case top.

Guitars were sold in department stores, passed around and traded like good stories, had their own display in pawnshops. Pretty soon, as the '70s tolled their way to that ultimate in slash chord reductionism, punk rock, it seemed like every bed had a guitar stashed under it. Sometimes they'd be taken out and played every day; sometimes they'd be found years later, with the tags still on.

Guitar lore galore.

I'm at a museum, very much like the one in Boston, only in a church basement on Manhattan's East 12th Street. It's a semiannual guitar mart, but I'm not here to buy (well, maybe . . .).

Here's a beaten-up Byrdland, thin-line, from the late '50s. I like the way the fingerboard comes to a point as it joins the body. Here's a Dan Armstrong, clear lucite; its weight makes my arm sag. I note the full two-octave fingerboard, the way the pickups can be quick-changed at will. It's next to a first-generation Ampeg electric bass, with a scroll top reminiscent of the behemoth instrument it was designed to emulate. Ampeg: amplified peg, the pickup located in the floor supporting rod.

I see a Paisley Telecaster from the late '60s. An Asian ESP shredder from the mid-'80s, with its headstock filed to a stiletto, tremolo clamped at the nut so that you can literally droop the strings off the neck and then yank them back in tune for the next suspended chord. A 1919 Martin 000-18 with later tuning pegs and steel strings, and a slight rub where the little finger of the picking hand anchors. A new Parker Fly. I can imagine each of their mating cries: the sitaresque D string drone; the blizzard of notes, two hands tapping on the neck; the slow ragtime fingerpick of pre-blues; the future's cybersonics. The people who play these musics and the music as it plays on them.

To immerse oneself in the guitar is to experience the panorama of our collective musical memory.

As for older instruments, highly individualized products of someone's acoustical imagination, this is as close as we'll get to reliving what they might have sounded like, pre-recording. Some are too fragile to string to pitch; we may not be able to revel in Antonio Stradivari's 1700 five-course guitar at standard A440, but we can try to fathom its voice by reading its rings, like the tree it once was. The young 'uns count off down the street in an hour. Catch them if you can.

The remarkable thing is that more than half a millennium of progress hasn't altered our conception of what a guitar can mean. Distorted by a vacuum tube or lightly brushed in a late-night bedroom, the guitar accommodates change without altering its basic nature; this is what gives these varied instruments their lifeline. No matter who picks it up when, the guitar will play the same song.

Yours.

NEW YORK CITY, APRIL 2000

Special thanks to César Díaz and Les Paul.

Baroque Guitars

BECAUSE OF THE GUITAR'S FRAGILITY, extremely few have survived from the instrument's earliest period, making it very difficult to trace its genealogy. Lack of standardized terminology in contemporary accounts further clouds its history. Nonetheless, in parts of Spain during the fifteenth century there was an instrument called the *vihuela*, depicted with a gently waisted shape like a guitar, but with stringing, tuning, repertoire, and social status more allied to the pear-shaped lute. Alongside the *vihuela* was another stringed instrument variously called a *guitarra* or *guiterne*, which was smaller in size and seems to have served a humbler role musically. Music historians continue to seek a more exact understanding of the evolution of these two species, but instruments that can properly be called guitars were in use in France and the Iberian Peninsula by the middle of the 1500s.

These early guitars were extremely light and delicate instruments with slender bodies and only slight waists. Initially they had four pairs of gut strings, but by the end of the sixteenth century five pairs became the norm and remained so until the late eighteenth century. This double stringing provided a rich tonal texture, but the Baroque guitar's gentle timbre, reminiscent of the lute, was far less powerful than that of the modern classical guitar. The frets on the fingerboard were also made of gut during this period, tied around the neck and adjustable in placement so as to achieve the best intonation. Like modern-day acoustic guitars, those from the Baroque era were appreciated for their portability and the fact that little musical ability was needed to produce a pleasant sound.

As with many other instruments, the early guitars that have been preserved through the ages are often exquisitely decorated. Some guitars were no doubt constructed in a more utilitarian manner, but most sophisticated art music of this period was produced under the patronage of the noble and wealthy, who naturally commissioned instruments befitting their tastes. All sorts of exotic and beautiful materials were used in their construction, including ebony, rosewood, ivory, mother-of-pearl, tortoiseshell, silver, and even gold. The surfaces were adorned with complex inlay, marquetry, and engraving. One of the most remarkable features was the treatment of the soundhole, inside which was a delicately carved rosette that was often gilded and painted. Although most of these precious guitars are now mute, their appearance echoes a glorious past.

GUITAR
Attributed to Belchior Dias
Portugal (Lisbon), about 1590

THIS INSTRUMENT IS CONSIDERED one of the earliest guitars known to have survived. The decoration is relatively spare overall, and the weight is heavy for a guitar of this size, but the workmanship is clearly that of an experienced craftsman. It might, in fact, have come from the same workshop as a much smaller guitar dated 1581, made by the Lisbon luthier Belchior Dias. By constructing the back from eight separate staves of wood, the maker was able to use pieces of a dark tropical wood (possibly rosewood) that would have been difficult to obtain in wider strips. Separating the staves with thin fillets of ivory creates an attractive graphic pattern. Like many early string instruments, this guitar has undergone considerable modification and repair during its history. The neck was relengthened and the entire top replaced in the twentieth century, but the geometric rose of laminated parchment is said to be original. Even with such drastic changes, this important instrument provides rare clues about the early features of guitar design.

A guitar is a woman to whom the saying, "Look but do not touch," does not apply; her rosette soundhole is the very opposite of a real rose bud, for she will not wither, no matter how much you touch her with your hands. On the contrary, when she is touched and played by a master hand, she will produce ever-new blossoms whose fragrant sonorities will please the ear.

— GASPAR SANZ

GUITAR

Jacopo Checchucci
Italy (Livorno), 1628

THE MAJORITY OF GUITARS surviving from the early 1600s were made in Italy, and most, like this instrument, are highly embellished. Working in the Tuscany region along the northwest coast, Jacopo Checchucci is undocumented except for his signature inside this exceptional guitar. He very likely trained in Venice, home to luthiers whose guitars exhibit similarly ornate decoration, especially the kind of scrolling designs covering this example. Like many early Italian guitars, the back of this instrument is vaulted rather than flat, constructed from individual curved staves of wood. The dark ebony back, sides, and neck provide a dramatic contrast with the ivory inlay. A bold pattern of ebony and ivory likewise frames the edges of the light spruce top and its soundhole, while delicate strips of ebony in arabesque patterns complete the composition. The gilded parchment rose set deep into the soundhole is especially fine on this guitar, with touches of red accentuating its separate tiers. Inlaid at the juncture of the neck and body is the silhouette of a double-headed eagle, a symbol of the Austrian House of Hapsburg, perhaps indicating that the original owner was a member of this royal family.

GUITAR
Attributed to Jakob Ertel
Italy (Rome), about 1690

MANY OF THE INSTRUMENT CRAFTSMEN who worked in seventeenth-century Italy were transplanted from German-speaking countries, especially from the area near a tiny town called Füssen in the foothills of the Bavarian Alps. Such was the case with Jakob Ertel, who Latinized his Christian name to Giacomo on his labels but retained his surname. Little else is known of Ertel, but he left behind at least one signed guitar and, apparently, this unlabeled instrument, both of which bear the same decorative treatment. Early Italian guitars were often covered with foliate designs, but geometric motifs were another obvious means of adorning large surfaces of an instrument. The sides, back, and neck of this handsome guitar are covered with a fine checkerboard pattern of ebony, fruitwood, ivory, and bone. Pearl squares outline the soundhole and top, creatively entwined into a tulip at the base. Much of the spruce top is left plain, however, as guitar makers generally feel that this acoustically active surface should not be too encumbered by unessential inlay.

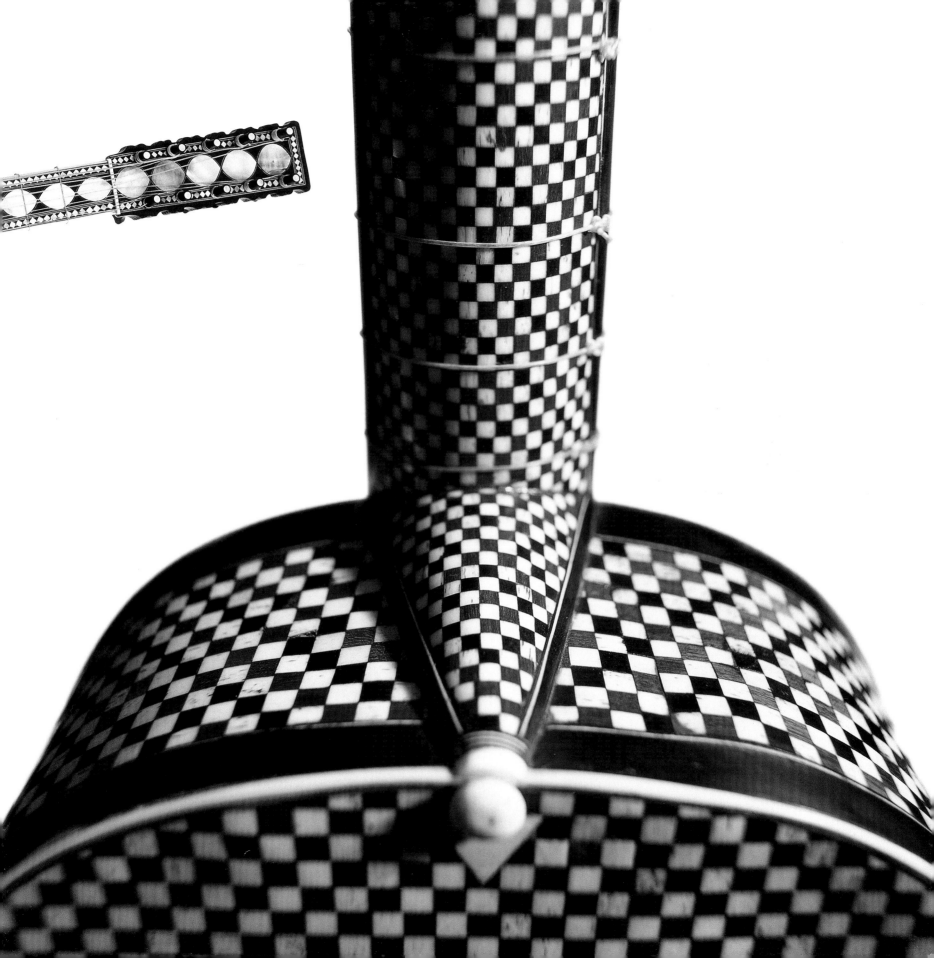

The enthusiasm of the King toward [this] music was such that the guitar became the most fashionable instrument. . . . Everyone at court wanted to learn, and God alone can imagine the universal scraping and plucking that ensued.

— MEMOIRS OF THE COUNT DE GRAMMONT

GUITAR
Nicholas Alexandre Voboam II (after 1633–about 1693)
France (Paris), 1680

GUITAR
Nicholas Alexandre Voboam II (after 1633–about 1693)
France (Paris), 1693

IT WAS NOT UNTIL THE 1640S that the guitar gained a foothold in France. When it did, King Louis XIV, a trendsetter in everything from music to fashion, became an avid player, though his technique was probably never more than basic. The so-called Sun King probably favored the guitar because it took less time to master than the lute, which by this period had accrued as many as eleven pairs of strings. For courtiers who wanted to stay in favor, the guitar became an essential accouterment of life at the royal French residences. Guitars were frequently depicted by artists such as Antoine Watteau, especially in the hands of stage actors. The French aristocracy's source for guitars that both looked and sounded harmonious was the Voboam family, at least four members of which were luthiers. This guitar is typical of the Voboams' fine work and the style of French makers in general, with roped edging of ebony and ivory, and a bridge that terminates in an upturned floral flourish called a moustache. The dark ebony sides are relieved with ivory stripes, while the convergence of similar stripes where the neck joins the body creates a splendid geometric device.

LONG BEFORE ENDANGERED SPECIES became a concern, tortoiseshell, with its vivid mottled patterns and satin surface, was an especially attractive material for beautifying precious objects. French instrument makers were frequent users of tortoiseshell, typically employing it as a veneer in geometric patterns on the sides and flat backs of their guitars. However ostentatious these veneered guitars might have been, they could not match this fantastic guitar made by Voboam, which is uniquely constructed from the entire carapace of a tortoise. Glazed ceramic replicas of the creature's head, tail, and feet have been added to complete the illusion. The instrument is more theatrical than musical, and the traditional waisted body shape has been necessarily dispensed with, but it was originally set up as a working guitar with five pairs of strings. About thirty surviving guitars by the Voboam family have been documented, but none quite so playful as this.

31

GUITAR
Antonio Stradivari (1644–1737)
Italy (Cremona), 1700

THE NAME STRADIVARI has always been synonymous with the finest-quality violins of the Baroque era. Few people are aware, however, that this venerated craftsman also made harps, mandolins, and guitars. The restrained but tasteful adornment on this lovely guitar allows one to appreciate its well-proportioned body, with a slightly wider lower bout and more accentuated waist than guitars of the previous century. As might be expected of a great violin maker, the wood selected for this guitar is excellent, from fine-grained spruce for the top to boldly striped maple on the back and sides. Contrasting with the light finish applied to the top, the back and sides exhibit a deep and glowing red-orange varnish that Stradivari began using on his violins near the end of the seventeenth century. This is one of only two documented guitars by Stradivari, but there may be one or two more privately owned in Italy.

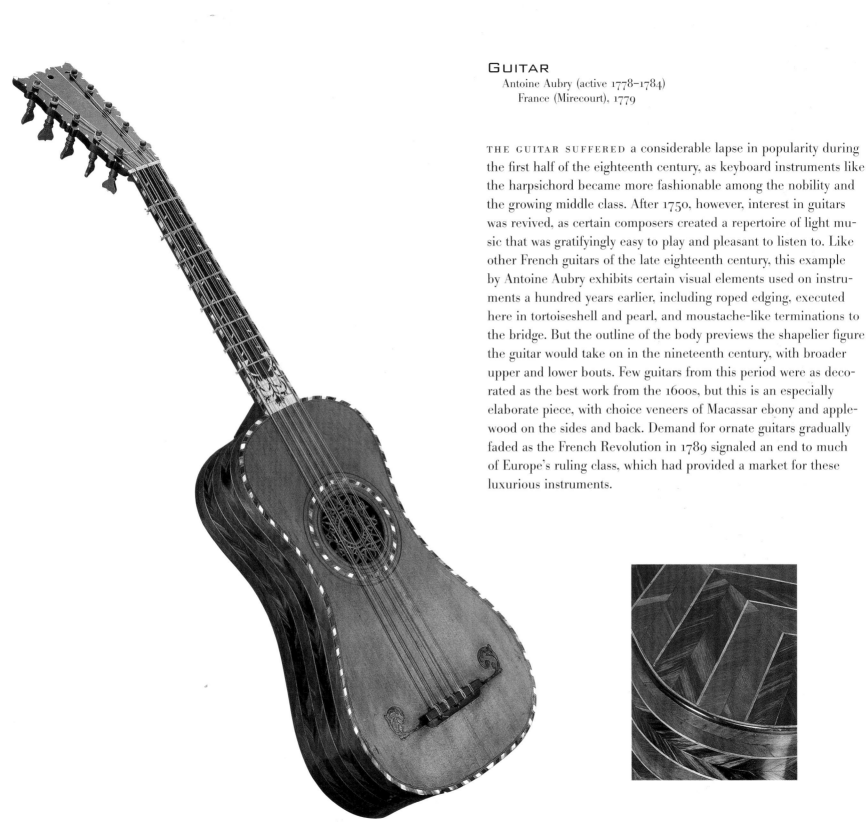

GUITAR
Antoine Aubry (active 1778–1784)
France (Mirecourt), 1779

THE GUITAR SUFFERED a considerable lapse in popularity during
the first half of the eighteenth century, as keyboard instruments like
the harpsichord became more fashionable among the nobility and
the growing middle class. After 1750, however, interest in guitars
was revived, as certain composers created a repertoire of light music that was gratifyingly easy to play and pleasant to listen to. Like
other French guitars of the late eighteenth century, this example
by Antoine Aubry exhibits certain visual elements used on instruments a hundred years earlier, including roped edging, executed
here in tortoiseshell and pearl, and moustache-like terminations to
the bridge. But the outline of the body previews the shapelier figure
the guitar would take on in the nineteenth century, with broader
upper and lower bouts. Few guitars from this period were as decorated as the best work from the 1600s, but this is an especially
elaborate piece, with choice veneers of Macassar ebony and applewood on the sides and back. Demand for ornate guitars gradually
faded as the French Revolution in 1789 signaled an end to much
of Europe's ruling class, which had provided a market for these
luxurious instruments.

BEGINNING IN THE LATE EIGHTEENTH CENTURY, the guitar experienced a number of significant changes, all contributing to the development of the modern classical instrument. Most visibly, six single strings replaced the five pairs that had been standard since the early 1600s, as tastes of the Classical and early Romantic periods dictated a clearer musical texture and expanded range. French and Italian guitar makers were the first to make six-string instruments, some as early as the 1770s. Spanish makers took a slightly different approach, first constructing guitars with six pairs of strings and only later reducing them to singles.

Guitar builders gradually introduced several other innovations that made for easier playing and improved tone and volume. The fingerboard was lengthened to give access to higher notes, and the frets were changed from gut tied around the neck to fixed metal or ivory strips. French makers introduced bridges in which the strings were held in place by wood or ivory pins (adopted from harp construction) rather than tied on. After about 1820, wood tuning pegs were gradually replaced by more reliable metal worm-gear "tuning machines." Some of the most important changes took place inside the guitar, as improved ways were sought to brace the thin softwood top. Traditionally, this surface had been reinforced with a few slender wood struts glued laterally to the underside, a method that many Italian and northern European makers continued to employ well into the nineteenth century. By the late 1750s, though, some progressive Spanish makers began applying struts to the lower portion of the top that were angled in a fan-like pattern. Further experiments with "fan bracing" eventually showed how positively such a system could affect the sound of the guitar.

The size and shape of the guitar (what the Spanish call its *plantilla*) were also gradually transformed during this period. The body became wider and larger, with a more pronounced waist and greater curvature in the upper and lower bouts. Within that general format makers produced a wide range of distinctive shapes, which often reflect the traditions of regional schools of building. Ornamentation became more restrained and was frequently limited to inlay (called binding or purfling) around the edges of the body and soundhole, to accentuate the guitar's outline. The soundhole was no longer filled with a decorative rose, but often the ends of the bridge were still terminated with an artistic flourish. Ultimately, much of the attractiveness of nineteenth-century guitars lies in a well-proportioned shape coupled with choice woods and a luxurious finish. Guitarists will argue that there is also great beauty in the sound.

GUITAR

Attributed to Gennaro Fabricatore I (active 1773–1832)
Italy (Naples), about 1805

THE MOST POPULAR string instrument in Naples during the second half of the eighteenth century was the wire-strung mandolin, but local luthiers like the Fabricatore family were also among the first to build six-string guitars, which were still gut-strung at this time. A common technique for dressing up early Neapolitan guitars was to imbed small pieces of pearl or ivory in a soft mixture of black or red resin called mastic, which then dried hard to hold the inlay in place. This is a relatively easy method for adorning a string instrument, and at a distance it creates a fairly ornate effect (close examination often reveals that the inlaid pieces are not cut very precisely). The inverted figure-eight headstock on this instrument mirrors the body's outline in miniature, and is a shape found on guitars throughout Europe in the early 1800s.

GUITAR

José Pagés (born 1762)
Spain (Cadiz), 1813

FROM THE LATE 1700S until the 1850s, the southern Spanish port of Cadiz was the country's preeminent center for guitar making. José (Josef) Pagés was one of the city's leading builders, and his work influenced other makers locally and abroad. This particular Pagés guitar is considered one of the finest of his surviving instruments, perhaps created as a presentation piece for an affluent customer. The top is inlaid with an abundance of elaborate foliate patterns executed in ebony and pearl, at a time when most Spanish makers were gradually reducing the number of frills on their guitar tops. But while the elegant decoration is somewhat old-fashioned for the period, the bracing system of this guitar is relatively progressive. Unlike many of its contemporaries, the top has five wood struts fanning out from the soundhole toward the bottom; this new system would prove vital in creating a powerful tone. Some Spanish guitar makers continued to use pairs of strings as late as the 1830s, long after other schools had changed to singles. This double stringing, with the greater volume it produced, provided a more effective accompaniment for Andalusian songs and dances.

38

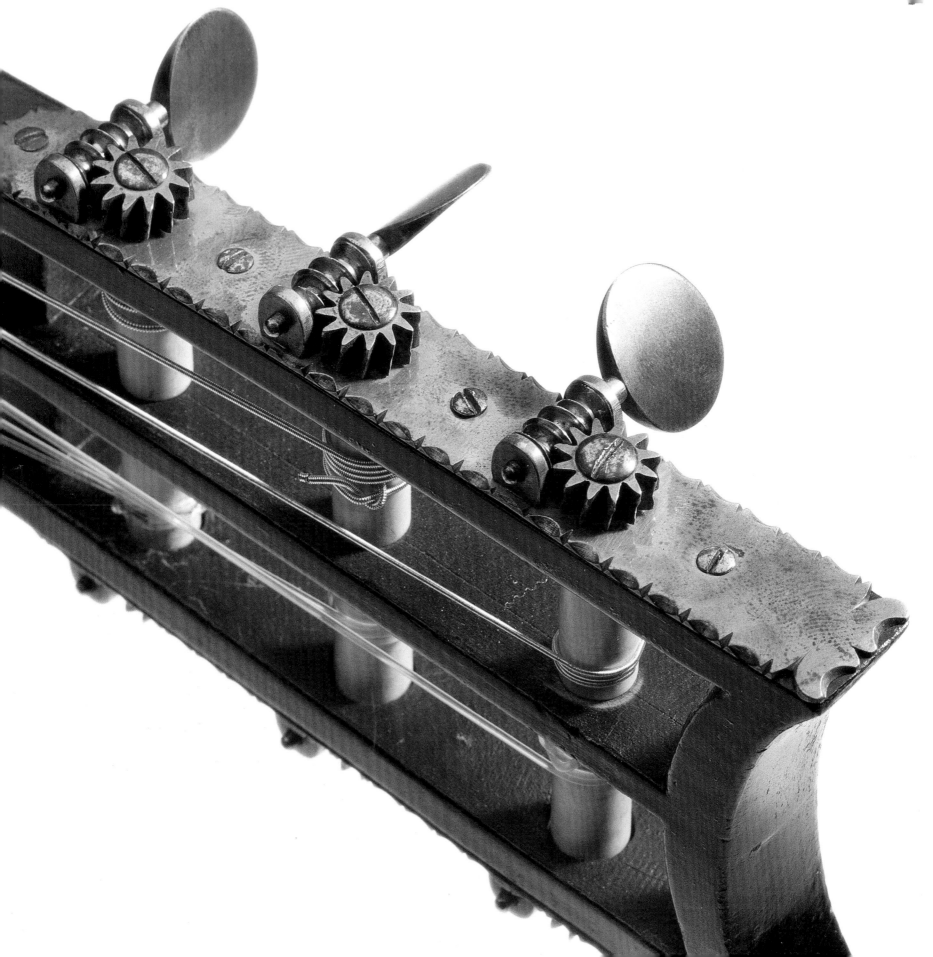

GUITAR

Louis Panormo (1784–1862)
England (London), 1823

ENGLAND HAD NO STRONG guitar tradition until the early nineteenth century, and what little demand that existed for guitars was
readily supplied by imports. All that gradually changed after the
1789 arrival of the Panormo family, instrument makers with roots in
Sicily. Vincenzo Panormo, the family patriarch, made mostly violins,
but his three sons became famous for their prolific output of guitars,
the quality of which was unsurpassed by any other English maker of
the nineteenth century. About 1819 they came into contact with the
internationally famous concert guitarist Fernando Sor (1778–1839),
who provided insightful advice as well as an opportunity to study
examples of fine Spanish guitars. The Panormos readily adopted a
Spanish body shape and system of fan bracing for their guitar tops,
and the eldest brother, Louis, advertised on his labels that he was
"the only maker of guitars in the Spanish style" (the only maker
outside of Spain, anyway). This early instrument exhibits a distinctive headstock design often used by the Panormos (and copied by
others), with a concave upper edge.

NINE-STRING GUITAR
René François Lacôte (1785–1855)
France (Paris), 1827

RENÉ FRANÇOIS LACÔTE was the most respected guitar maker in France during a period when much of the instrument's first serious repertoire was being created. He generally made six-string guitars, but several instruments survive from his shop with one or more additional bass strings lying off the fingerboard. This is one of several instruments made by Lacôte for guitarist Napoleon Coste, the most important French guitar virtuoso of the nineteenth century, whose performing career ended suddenly at age fifty-seven when he broke his right arm. Even today guitarists often crave notes that are lower than their E string, and the three extra basses on this Lacôte nine-stringer would have provided Coste with some wonderfully sonorous tones to enrich his playing. This guitar was further customized with a special bridge that allows the strings to be tied to the end of the body, and also with a long oval piece of maple attached to the top where the little finger of the right hand can rest. Resting this finger on the top was not an unusual playing technique in the nineteenth century, but is generally frowned upon by today's classical guitarists. Except for its wide, organically contoured headstock, the other features of this guitar are typical of Lacôte's style, such as the multilayered ebony and whalebone binding around the edges.

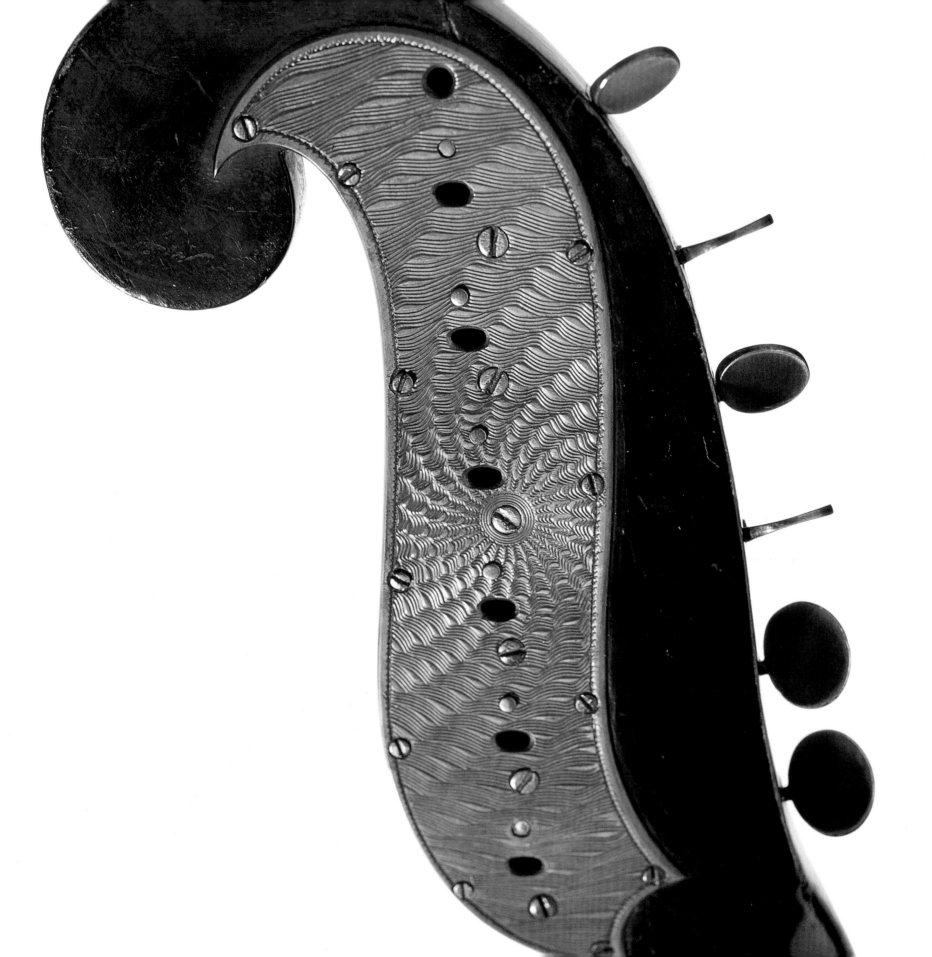

GUITAR

Johann Georg Stauffer (1778–1853)
Austria (Vienna), about 1830

SEVERAL GUITAR INNOVATIONS are credited to Johann Georg
Stauffer. Many of these were adopted by other German-speaking
makers, including some who carried the ideas to America. Stauffer's
two most notable improvements were a neck whose angle can be
adjusted with a clock-key wrench, and an extended fingerboard that
floats slightly above the surface of the body. Earlier guitar necks
were rigidly fixed, making any change in alignment a difficult proce-
dure. A floating fingerboard allowed more of the top to vibrate, and
its extended length gave access to higher notes. Stauffer supposedly
worked out these features with Italian guitar virtuoso Luigi Legnani
(1790–1877), and many Stauffer instruments bear a label specifying
them as a Legnani model. Composer Franz Schubert (1797–1828)
is believed to have owned a Stauffer guitar, and also wrote for an
unusual bowed guitar called an *arpeggione*, invented by Stauffer
in 1823. A visual characteristic associated with Stauffer guitars is a
headstock shaped as a sideways scroll with all of the tuning pegs
along one side. This feature and a shallow body with very rounded
bouts became common traits of German guitar design throughout
the nineteenth century.

Guitar

Christian Frederick Martin (1796–1873)
United States (New York, New York), 1833–1840

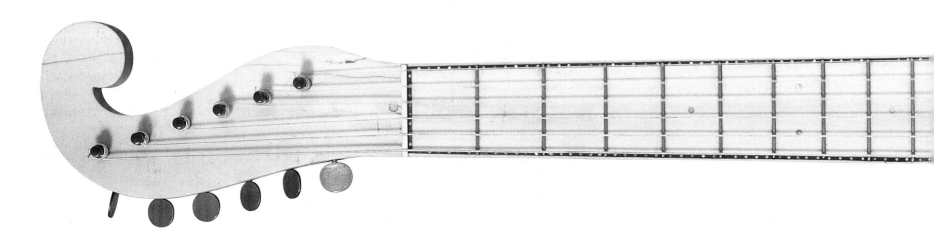

THIS INSTRUMENT IS ONE of the prettiest American guitars of the nineteenth century. Its maker, Christian Frederick Martin, was born in the instrument-making center of Markneukirchen in Germany's Saxony region. Although concrete proof is lacking, tradition holds that Martin was an apprentice and later shop foreman for the inventive Viennese guitar maker J. G. Stauffer. What is known for certain is that Martin immigrated to the United States in 1833, where he soon became the country's first influential guitar maker, creating a manufactory that remains world famous to this day. Dainty by today's standards, this instrument is the type of "parlor" guitar Martin first produced after coming to America, and it does indeed include features of Stauffer's work, such as the sideways-scroll headstock and adjustable neck. The use of so much ivory on an American guitar is exceptional during this period, especially for the neck. Combined with the "thumbprint" inlays of pearl and abalone around the top, the effect is almost jewelry-like, an aesthetic that would have appealed to young female players, who constituted an important element of guitar ownership in antebellum America.

GUITAR

Probably by Antoine Anciaume (born 1776)
France (Mirecourt), about 1840

MOMENTOUS HISTORICAL EVENTS have long been commemo-
rated with the creation of artistic objects, whether a triumphal arch
or a silver tray. This wondrously ornate guitar was constructed about
1840 to honor the transfer of the remains of Napoleon Bonaparte
(1769–1821) from his grave on the island of St. Helena into Paris,
the so-called *retour des cendres* (return of the ashes). The instrument is encrusted with emblems and scenes celebrating the emperor's military career, all executed in engraved pieces of pearl and
iridescent abalone. The soundhole cradles a restful scene of his
tomb on St. Helena, surrounded by oval cartouches depicting important sites in Napoleonic history, from Waterloo to Elba. The
fingerboard imitates the Colonne Vendôme in Paris, with an architectural base, spirals embellished with battle scenes, and a statue
of Napoleon in campaign attire. A stylized sun atop the headstock
shines down on the self-proclaimed emperor. The bridge terminates
in lightning bolts, while centered below is a Legion of Honor star
holding a tiny red gemstone. The Anciaume family worked in Mirecourt, a town in the northeastern French province of Vosges with a
long tradition of making string instruments. They were not among
Europe's best-known luthiers, but this presentation guitar may have
been produced especially for display at a trade exhibition.

48

BAMBINA GUITAR
Possibly by D. & A. Roudhloff
England (London), about 1870

GUITARIST AND CHILD PRODIGY Catharina Josepha Pelzer was better known as Madame Sidney Pratten after her marriage to a concert flutist in 1854 at the age of thirty-three. She had moved with her family to England from Germany about 1829 and was already giving recitals there by the age of ten, having been taught by her father, Ferdinand Pelzer, a noted guitarist in his own right. Precocious musicians especially intrigued London concertgoers, and Catharina Pelzer was one of the city's best-loved performers, later establishing herself as a teacher with clientele that included members of British nobility. As a child, Madame Pratten had played on a small "terz" guitar, so called because it was tuned a tone and a half (or three steps) above the normal instrument. For her youngest pupils, Pratten developed a small octave-pitched instrument she called the *bambina* (baby) guitar. Resting in its original burled walnut case with green satin lining, this *bambina* guitar once belonged to Madame Pratten herself.

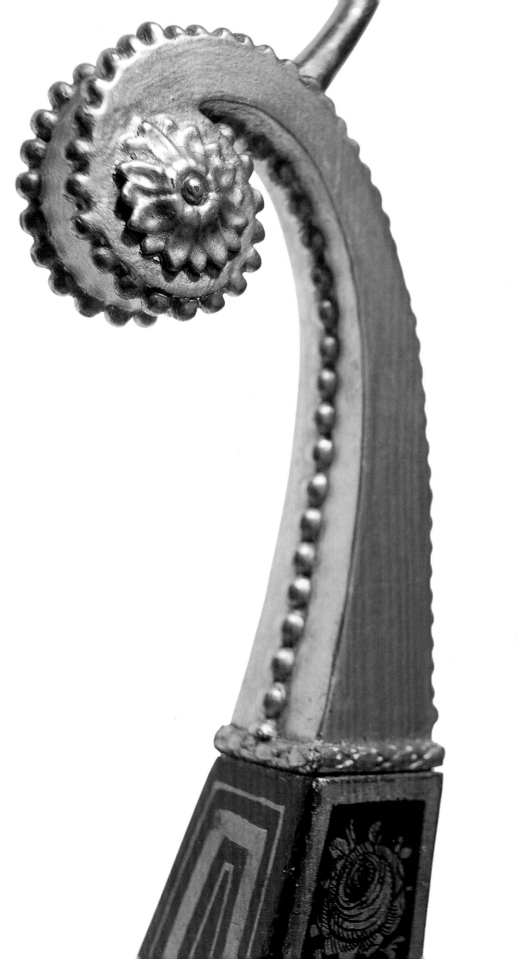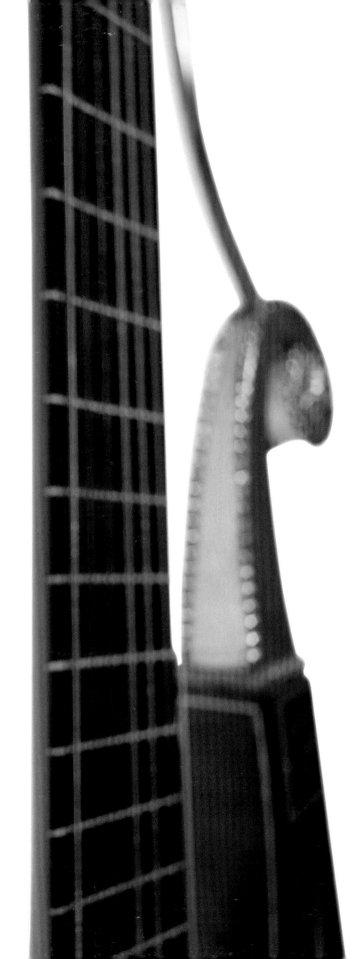

Lyre Guitars and Other Hybrids

ARTISTS HAVE BEEN COPYING and adapting the architectural and sculptural forms of ancient Greece and Rome since the Renaissance. But emulation of the artifacts and fashions of the classical world became especially strong in the late eighteenth and early nineteenth century, as many important archaeological and artistic works from antiquity were rediscovered. The design and ornamentation of musical instruments were not exempt from this fad, and pianos and harps were dressed up with motifs borrowed from classical civilization.

The lyre was a particularly popular decorative motif, so the adaptation of its shape to the guitar was perhaps inevitable. Lyre guitars were made in many parts of Europe, but they were prevalent in France. With a sound cavity configured differently than the normal guitar, these lyre-type instruments supposedly produced a deeper and slightly louder tone, but one that was rather dull. The presence of arms along each side of the neck in all of the various styles of lyre guitars made them awkward to play. The flat base on many examples, though, allowed them to serve a more meaningful purpose, which was as decorative objects that could be displayed in the drawing room, a proud indication of the owner's social status and interest in the fine arts.

The lyre guitar was the most popular instrument inspired by classicism, but many other plucked string instruments were created that incorporated features of this style. Among these were several hyphenated hybrid instruments with names such as guitar-harp and harp-lute-guitar. Most of these were marketed to female amateurs, who employed them for simple tunes or to provide basic chordal accompaniment to popular songs. Professional guitarists were understandably antagonistic toward these novelties, but their fears were unfounded, as the vogue for such instruments was ultimately short-lived.

LYRE GUITAR
Probably by François Gratel (born 1793)
France (Mirecourt), about 1810

THE FRENCH WERE THE MOST PROLIFIC makers of lyre guitars,
and at least one style-conscious luthier was already making them by
1785. But it was between 1805 and 1815 that they experienced their
greatest popularity. This lovely instrument by Gratel (owned by rock
guitarist Steve Howe) exhibits the most classic form, with slender,
graceful arms connected to the headstock by a gilded brass yoke. It
is an especially ornate example, with small pearl dots accentuating
its elegant outline. Double soundholes with comma-shaped inserts
are also typical of French lyre guitars, and serve to reinforce the
form's balanced symmetry. Lyre guitars were only a passing fashion,
but it should be noted that even the earliest examples consistently
have six single strings at a time when such an arrangement had not
yet become standard on the regular guitar. Whether this had any
influence on mainstream guitarists is uncertain, but as six strings
became the norm, lyre guitars lost even this small advantage and
were soon considered as antiquated as the ancient Greek instruments that inspired them.

LYRE GUITAR
Pons fils
France (Paris), about 1810

THIS MAJESTIC GUITAR takes a decidedly architectural approach to the lyre form, with stately wood columns supporting a gilded yoke that terminates in exuberant spirals. This model is no more useful for music making than any other lyre guitar, but the furniture-like appearance would have greatly enhanced its appeal as a piece of interior decoration. A lyre guitar provided a most attractive fashion accessory for an affluent young woman, who might pose with it for a painted portrait, dressed in a costume emulating that of an ancient Greek musician. When actually trying to play such a clumsy instrument, though, her posture would have been far from graceful. In an age when personal decorum was supremely important among well-bred debutantes, this may have contributed to the relatively brief fashion for lyre guitars.

53

LYRE GUITAR
(Apollo lyre)
Clementi and Company
England (London), about 1810

THE LACK OF A GUITAR-PLAYING tradition in the British Isles may have contributed to the English interest in neoclassical-styled guitars. For the many different hybrid string instruments they produced during the early nineteenth century, the English preferred a dark finish covering much of the body, trimmed with gilded ornaments like the acanthus leaves around the edges of this instrument. This style of ornamentation is somewhat reminiscent of the eighteenth-century French technique of lacquer work called *vernis martin*. The body of this lyre guitar reads strongly as a crescent moon, a universally popular symbol, although the use of this shape may also reflect early nineteenth-century Europe's strong interest in Turkish motifs, among which the crescent was a prevalent figure. As a foil to the dark of the moon there is also the light of the sun, here represented by a gilded likeness of Apollo, who adorns a hinged disk partially covering the metal tuning pins.

54

GUITAR-HARP

Mordaunt Levien
France (Paris), about 1825

MANY YOUNG EUROPEAN and American women of the nineteenth century aspired to play the harp. The sound was beautiful, the appearance elegant, and it was one of the few instruments considered appropriate for females because no unseemly posture or facial distortion was required to play it (for this reason, instruments such as the cello or horn were out of the question). If one could not afford a harp or summon the patience to master it, there was the guitar-harp, which offered a vaguely harp-like sound and portability besides. London-based music professor Mordaunt Levien took out a patent for his *guitare-harpe* in France in 1825, and probably had his instruments constructed there as well. The strings are tuned to an open C chord and, by pressing the left thumb on the small brass studs projecting through the back of the neck, one could raise the pitch of selected strings to avoid difficult fingering in certain passages. The mechanism operates similarly to the pedals on period harps, and Levien even refers to these studs as pedals in his patent. Although less embellished than some lyre guitars of a decade earlier, this guitar-harp still shows classical influence, with a gilded face of Apollo surrounded by sunbeams on the headstock.

Harp-guitar

Joseph Laurent Mast (active 1802–1830)
France (Toulouse), 1827

THE TERM "HARP-GUITAR" has been applied to a variety of musical instruments from the early nineteenth century to the present, but seldom as accurately as with this French creation. Here, a six-string guitar neck is cleverly mounted to a harp-shaped body, which includes a characteristic fluted column. The strings of a true harp intersect its hollow, resonant body at an oblique angle, but on this crossbred instrument the strings lie parallel to the wood's surface, as is typical of guitars. It is a little surprising that the maker did not add any extra, openly tuned strings to the side of the fingerboard, a common feature of other harp-guitars. Presumably this composite experiment was played in a vertical position, resting on its base. This would free the player from having to support the instrument, but would also require a rather unusual playing posture. Mast was a maker of both violins and guitars, the backs of which he sometimes embellished with female figures. It is unknown whether his harp-guitar was intended to possess a unique tone quality, but he certainly succeeded in fashioning an object with unusual visual appeal.

HARP-GUITAR
Emilius Nicolai Scherr (1794–1874)
United States (Philadelphia, Pennsylvania), 1830s

ALTHOUGH MOST SUCCESSFUL as a maker of pianos and organs, a skill he had studied in his native Denmark, Emilius Scherr patented his unusual-looking harp-guitar in 1831, nine years after emigrating to Philadelphia. For its "good and sweet tone," Scherr received a premium award at an 1832 trade exhibition held by Philadelphia's Franklin Institute. But the design slipped into oblivion soon thereafter, and only five surviving examples have been located. The body of this guitar might best be described as spoon-shaped, but Scherr's patent covered guitars of any form in which the lower end rested on the floor, this being the instrument's only real harp-like aspect. Like a few other guitar makers who worked before and after him, Scherr apparently felt that freeing the player from physically supporting the guitar would be a great advantage. He may have also reasoned that not holding the instrument's body too close would make for a clearer tone. The use of gilded figures and striping on the back is similar to the treatment of high-style Philadelphia furniture of the period, and is characteristic of a slightly later form of classicism from the 1830s called Empire Style.

HARPO-LYRE

André Augustin Chévrier (active 1820–1842)
France (Paris), about 1830

POP MUSIC FANS typically associate multiple-neck guitars with
rock stars of the 1970s, so it may come as a surprise that instruments like this impressive triple-neck guitar were introduced 140
years earlier. Music professor Jean-François Salomon, who worked
in the French city of Besançon, patented a harpo-lyre in 1829,
whose two extra necks suggest the shape of lyre guitars that had
enjoyed a brief vogue twenty years earlier. Regarding the harpo-lyre,
a contemporary reviewer stated that "it is scarcely possible to describe bounds to the effects which may be derived from it." In spite
of this laudatory endorsement and a careful reading of Salomon's
patent text, it is still unclear exactly how the player was supposed
to use the extra necks, since the suggested tuning of their strings
does not lend itself to playing chords. The most fascinating part of
Salomon's patent is his vague description of how the harpo-lyre can
be linked with two slender metal arms to a freestanding resonating
box. This mysterious box was intended to amplify the harpo-lyre's
sound and, through means not described in detail, to provide "cre-
scendo, diminuendo, tremolo, and bass drum" by way of four pedals.

58

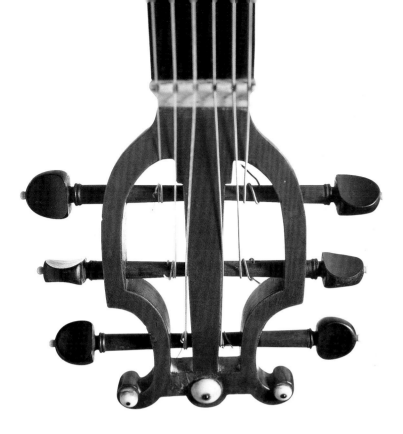

WAPPENGITARRE
(shield-shaped guitar)
Probably by Victorin Drassegg (1782–1847)
Austria (Bregenz), about 1835

THE FASHION FOR LYRE-SHAPED guitars was short-lived, but
the lyre continued to be a popular artistic conceit used on musical
instruments into the twentieth century. On this shield-shaped
Wappengitarre, a lyre is creatively integrated as a headstock design.
The instrument's peculiar body shape is found principally in Alpine
regions, and might be described as festooned. It is veneered on all
surfaces with attractive burled walnut over a pine substrate. Born in
the Moravian (now Czech Republic) town of Velká Poloma, Victorin
Drassegg began his career as a wood joiner. Pressed into military
service against his will, and captured by the French in Italy, he escaped to carry on his life under the name Friedrich Grünwald in
the Austrian town of Bregenz, at the eastern end of Lake Constance.
With a plentiful supply of fine wood, many of the areas bordering
the Alps have distinguished traditions of string instrument making.
The guitars and zithers made by Drassegg are considered to be of
good but not great quality, although he is said to have been an
excellent player.

The Modern Classical and Flamenco Guitar

SINCE ITS EARLIEST HISTORY the guitar has been closely associated with Spain, and it is considered the country's national instrument in much the same way that the harp is allied with Ireland. It should come as no surprise, then, that classical and flamenco guitars as we now know them are largely the result of developments and refinements made by Spanish guitar makers working from the mid-nineteenth through the early twentieth centuries.

Scholarship has traditionally pointed to Antonio de Torres as the man who, in the 1850s, was responsible for transforming the guitar from a relatively petite "parlor" instrument to the larger-bodied classical model of today. With only slight variations, the size and shape of guitar body that Torres standardized has been used by classical guitar makers for the past 150 years. Although Torres produced guitars of varying quality and price, his best work set a new standard for construction quality, and his instruments outclassed those of virtually all other guitar makers until the late nineteenth century. For bracing the underside of his guitar tops, Torres adopted the basic fan-pattern of struts that had already been developed by Spanish makers in the late eighteenth century. But he refined this bracing system to produce instruments with a strong, rich sound and a wide range of dynamic response. Ultimately, Torres's success was less a result of introducing new ideas to the guitar than of realizing the potential of several that had been used previously.

Torres had no direct successor, but his ideas were readily embraced by successive generations of Spanish guitar builders, who further elevated the craft to create a golden age of classical guitar making in the early twentieth century. Their knowledge has in turn been passed along to a present generation of makers working throughout the world, which today provides guitar buyers with a fine selection of instruments from which to choose. Like their predecessors, these skilled artisans strive to create guitars that are lovely to behold but even more beautiful to hear. As with the violin, both players and makers of the classical guitar have been generally resistant to ideas that stray too far from those that have proven successful for more than a century, and so the design of the classical guitar has indeed become classic.

The guitar is a perfect instrument for subtle tonal variations. The guitar's nearly infinite number of sound colors is almost orchestral.
— JULIAN BREAM

FLAMENCO GUITAR
Antonio de Torres (1817–1892)
Spain (Seville), about 1858

BORN NEAR ALMERÍA, along Spain's southern Mediterranean coast, Antonio de Torres moved to Seville in 1845, and there he is believed to have developed a model that became the archetype for all classical guitars. His instruments were played by many fine musicians, but the most celebrated was the Spanish virtuoso Francisco Tárrega, who greatly improved the approach to both guitar playing and repertoire. Torres generally concentrated his efforts on those aspects of guitar construction that most affect tone, and he seldom added more than the simplest of decoration. This modest-looking guitar is one of the earliest from his shop. Although somewhat smaller than most modern classical guitars, it shows the basic shape that Torres is credited with creating. Given the heavy wear on the top of the instrument, it was probably used for flamenco playing, the player percussively striking the soft spruce surface with his fingers.

FLAMENCO GUITAR
Santos Hernández (1874–1943)
Spain (Madrid), 1934

THE DEMARCATION BETWEEN classical and flamenco guitars was formerly much less clear than it is today. In Spain a player simply purchased the best affordable instrument. For the Gypsies who played flamenco music this was typically a guitar made from indigenous cypress wood, with old-fashioned wood tuning pegs rather than state-of-the-art metal geared tuners. Over time these specifications gradually became codified as features particular to the flamenco guitar, although there are frequent exceptions among modern instruments. Performers, however, still recognize that lightweight cypress wood provides a lively tonal response that is well suited to the percussive qualities of flamenco playing. Santos Hernández was the most respected maker of flamenco guitars in the early twentieth century. His instruments were in great demand, and good examples are now very difficult to find because players have virtually worn them out. The thin plastic plates applied along each side of the soundhole on this guitar, called *golpeadores* (tap plates), protect the softwood top from the rhythmic drumming of the player's fingers, a feature unique to flamenco guitar music.

CLASSICAL GUITAR
Hermann Hauser I (1882–1952)
Germany (Munich), 1928

HERMANN HAUSER I was the first non-Spanish guitar builder to acquire international fame for his work, especially after Andrés Segovia began using an instrument of his for concert performances in the late 1930s. Hauser studied the guitar designs of Antonio de Torres, but applied "his Teutonic engineering principles" to their construction (to quote guitarist Julian Bream). Many consider his significance as a guitar maker to be rivaled only by Torres. Hauser's guitars are a bit small by today's standards, but are of extremely high quality and demonstrate that bigger is not necessarily better in achieving great tonal carrying power. Performers find Hauser's guitars to be extremely versatile, good for playing not only classical music but also folk and jazz. His use of exceptionally good tone woods, combined with subtle refinements in bracing the top, resulted in instruments with a wide yet balanced dynamic range and a broad palette of tone color.

CLASSICAL GUITAR

Francisco Simplicio (1874–1932/3)
Spain (Barcelona), about 1929–30

AT ONE TIME BARCELONA was second in importance only to
Madrid as a center of classical guitar making. The city's current
school of building can be traced to Enrique García (1868–1922),
who opened a shop there in the early 1890s after learning his trade
in Madrid. Francisco Simplicio carried on the traditions of García
and, as his only student, became successor to his shop. Barcelona
makers often embellished their guitar headstocks with foliate
carving, as in the present example. This instrument also exhibits
Simplicio's tendency to make fancy guitars with wide, elaborate
binding, many of which were sold to wealthy Spanish expatriates
living in Latin America who had made their fortune in the Rio de
La Plata area near Buenos Aires and Montevideo. Although not
visible, the interior workmanship of Simplicio's guitars is particularly precise, perhaps a result of his earlier training as a furniture
maker. About 1929, Simplicio conceived the radical notion of moving the soundhole farther up the body and straddling the fingerboard, which he reasoned would allow more of the top to be
acoustically active. Although some leading players praised this
improvement, it did not receive widespread acceptance, and
Simplicio produced only nine guitars of this model.

Turn-of-the-Century Guitars

THROUGHOUT MUCH OF THE NINETEENTH CENTURY the guitar led a dignified but sedate existence. As had always been the case, people continued to play guitars for personal enjoyment and for informal gatherings in the parlor or salon. The proportions of the classical gut-strung guitar were more or less standardized by about 1860, and there were many European and American composers (usually guitarists themselves) who created a substantial and often challenging repertoire for the instrument. But this realm of serious music was still a very limited one, as the guitar could not compete successfully with the long-standing popularity of instruments such as the violin and piano.

The forty years straddling the year 1900 constituted a very fertile period of human imagination and innovation. The guitar, too, began to undergo significant changes during this era as its popularity swelled to tremendous proportions. In the early twentieth century, an increasingly industrialized society allowed people more leisure time for pursuits such as music, and a little more cash to purchase something as extravagant as a musical instrument. Plucked-string instruments such as the mandolin and banjo were especially popular, and the demand for guitars gradually increased as well. Manufacturers responded by producing more diverse styles of instruments with a range of prices to suit every buyer, and illustrated catalogs soon became a common and persuasive means of advertising. With a prosperous economy and broad consumer base, the United States became the world's dominant force in guitar design and manufacture throughout the twentieth century.

Although certain innovations in guitar design at the turn of the century were forward looking, instrument makers were generally a conservative lot, often sticking with the same tried-and-true methods and materials used by their predecessors. Even the decorative schemes employed on guitars during this period were frequently derived from motifs used in much earlier times. Two developments in guitar construction during the late nineteenth century are of particular note. The first was the introduction of models that used steel strings rather than gut, producing a new type of guitar with a louder and brighter tone. The second was the creation of the arch-top guitar. The top and back of these guitars are carved with arched contours like those on the violin, which had a considerable effect on volume and tone color. It would be several years after their introduction before either of these ideas would receive widespread adoption, but they would both prove to be of long-lasting importance.

WILLIAM B. TILTON, a teacher and performer active in New York and Boston, took out four patents in the 1850s relating to guitar construction, two of which were intended to create a freer tone. One of these patents was for a longitudinal wooden brace inside the body, designed to lessen stress on the top as a structural member. The second involved fastening the strings to a metal tailpiece at the bottom of the body rather than attaching them directly to the bridge. Tilton also took out a design patent for placing a stamped metal disk in the soundhole, as seen in this instrument: a strictly nonfunctional feature. The main purpose of this medallion is to help disguise Tilton's wooden brace, which would be visually distracting if it were completely exposed. Another unusual aspect of Tilton-model guitars is that the grain of their spruce tops is oriented diagonally across the body. Although this is not a patented feature, here too Tilton was probably trying to improve the tone quality in some way. This particular guitar is a deluxe example of the Tilton model distributed by Haynes and Company in Boston, with artistic fingerboard inlay presumably done by Pehr Anderberg, a Swedish craftsman who oversaw the firm's guitar factory.

FLAT-TOP GUITAR
Probably by Lyon and Healy (Washburn brand)
United States (Chicago, Illinois), about 1900

FOUNDED IN 1864, Chicago's Lyon and Healy company was America's largest distributor of all kinds of musical instruments at the end of the nineteenth century, claiming an annual production of over 100,000 Washburn-brand guitars, mandolins, and zithers. They sold a wide range of guitars at all price levels, but also offered models that were far fancier than those of nearly any other American company. Although unlabeled, this unique guitar was likely a custom order from Lyon and Healy, as certain details bear similarity to their high-end instruments. Whereas the fingerboard inlay on other ornate guitars and banjos from this period typically shows symmetrical patterns in a classical style, it was clearly the Art Nouveau movement that inspired the bold, asymmetrical leaves on this instrument. There are many other pleasing touches throughout the guitar, from the artistic engraving in the pearl inlay to the ornamental flourishes that terminate the light wood inlay on the rosewood sides. As the twentieth century progressed, and less expensive guitars began to be offered, most buyers became less interested in paying for a spectacular piece like this one.

Arch-top guitar
Orville H. Gibson (1856–1918)
United States (Kalamazoo, Michigan), about 1900

ORVILLE GIBSON IS GENERALLY credited as the first to carve the
top and back of a guitar into an arched shape rather than making
them flat, as they had traditionally been. He first applied this idea in
the 1880s to the mandolin, which was experiencing great popularity
at the time. But while violin makers construct the sides of their
instruments from thin wood pieces bent to shape, Gibson sawed out
the sinuous sides from a solid piece of wood in order to avoid dis-
rupting the natural growth direction of the grain. Any acoustical
gain from this labor-intensive process was marginal at best, and the
Gibson Company did not adopt this practice for their later production models. This guitar is one of a handful of surviving instruments
made by Orville Gibson before 1902, when a group of investors
bought his business. It is typical of his style, with a steep arch along
the top and back, curving abruptly into a large, flat expanse in the
center. The guitar is surprisingly lightweight, the result of careful
thinning of all the body's surfaces. Despite such attention to detail,
the tone of Orville Gibson's guitars is considered somewhat dull by
modern standards.

ARCH-TOP GUITAR

(Style O Artist)
Gibson Mandolin-Guitar Company
United States (Kalamazoo, Michigan), about 1918

THE GIBSON COMPANY's first commercial arch-top guitar was their Style O, featuring a traditional guitar outline and large oval sound-hole. In 1908 they modified this model to one referred to as the Style O Artist, incorporating a stylish scroll on the bass side of the body and a flat cutaway area on the treble side, terminating in a jaunty point. The scroll shape is copied directly from Gibson's popular Style F mandolins of the period, and is made hollow to provide an additional resonating cavity. Orville Gibson had similarly tried to enhance the sonority of his early guitars by making a portion of their necks hollow, but this created weakness at a critical juncture, and the idea was not incorporated into later instruments. Although the scroll and cutaway serve musical purposes, the flamboyant styling represents an early instance of a commercially made guitar being altered primarily to create a new and distinctive look. The design similarities between early Gibson guitars and the company's mandolins were intentional, as the guitar's main role was to provide bass and chordal accompaniment in the mandolin orchestras that were so popular in America during the early 1900s. The guitar likewise took second billing in the company's full name, which at the time was the Gibson Mandolin-Guitar Company.

Arch-top guitar with sympathetic strings

Joseph Bohmann (1848–about 1930)
United States (Chicago, Illinois), about 1910

BOHEMIAN-BORN JOSEPH BOHMANN was one of countless European instrument makers who immigrated to America during the nineteenth century, bringing with them a wonderfully distinctive approach to their craft. Primarily a violin maker, Bohmann arrived in the United States in 1873, and in 1876 established a large factory in Chicago, where he produced all sorts of string instruments, including what may have been the first American-made mandolins. His labels boldly proclaim him as "The World's Greatest Musical Instrument Maker" and display various medals he had won at international exhibitions. This unusual Bohmann guitar has six additional strings inside the body, intended to pick up vibrations from the six regular strings and add their own subtle flavor to the tonal mix. So-called sympathetic strings have been used only occasionally on European and American plucked string instruments, but they are more common in types from south Asia, such as the sitar. Bohmann has also employed a peculiar body shape, and his quirky style is further evident in the curious mix of unconventional shapes inlaid as fret markers.

Harp Guitars

INSTRUMENT MAKERS HAVE OFTEN SEARCHED for ways to extend the musical range of their creations, and guitars have not been exempt from the process. By the late sixteenth century lute makers were placing long extra strings to the side of the fingerboard, which could be tuned to desired bass pitches and plucked with the right thumb. In the late eighteenth century guitars began to follow suit, and since that time numerous designs have been developed that provide extra "harp" strings on a guitar. Since the harp guitar has no distinct repertoire, its extra strings are tuned and played ad libitum to support whatever musical style is being rendered. Ostensibly, a guitarist could use these extra strings to better perform lute music that calls for especially low bass notes, but this seems not to have been done with much regularity. Low-pitched "harp" strings primarily add a deep, sonorous quality to the guitar's overall tone by reverberating sympathetically in response to the vibrations of the main strings.

The incorporation of extra bass strings onto a guitar almost always gives birth to an interesting-looking instrument. The body is typically wider than normal instruments to accommodate the greater number of strings, creating a frame whose size alone attracts attention. Then there is the need to attach the harp strings to some structure other than a regular headstock. If only a few harp strings are used, the headstock can sometimes be widened enough to accommodate them. However, when five or more strings are added, harp guitars often take on more dramatic shapes, with structural supports that would make an engineer envious. The manufacture of harp guitars over the past two centuries has been fitful at best, but their inherent oddness never ceases to fascinate even the nonmusical.

HARP GUITAR
C. F. Martin and Company
United States (Nazareth, Pennsylvania), about 1850–60

C. F. MARTIN AND COMPANY has never been known for eccentric guitar designs, but someone working in their shop in the mid-nineteenth century produced what must be one of the earliest harp guitars made in the United States. It was not until the beginning of the twentieth century that harp guitars experienced any real vogue in America, and even then Martin took only a limited interest in such instruments, producing about ten examples between 1902 and 1912, with anywhere from ten to eighteen extra strings. The scrolling headstock on this remarkably early instrument has been made extra wide to carry both the six regular and the four extra bass strings. A simple wood strut resting on a flattened area at the upper end of the body supports the off-kilter layout. Apart from these necessary modifications, the guitar shows the humble trimmings that have long characterized Martin products, like the thin herringbone inlay around the soundhole. This one-of-a-kind harp guitar was discovered in 1997, abandoned in a Mississippi farm building, but has received careful cosmetic restoration by its new owners.

HARP GUITAR

(Style U)
Gibson Mandolin-Guitar Company
United States (Kalamazoo, Michigan), 1920

ALTHOUGH NOT AN ESPECIALLY rare instrument, the large size and bold styling of the Gibson Style U harp guitar always commands awe. As with all early Gibson instruments, the top and back are arched; the so-called Florentine curve on the upper part of the body is also found on many of the company's other models. Like the smaller, six-stringed Style O Artist guitar, the Style U was meant for use in mandolin orchestras, harmonically supporting the tinkly melodies played by its higher-pitched cousins. The numerous sub-bass strings allowed the player to further augment the music with a sonorous bass line. Early Gibson harp guitars had as many as twelve bass strings, but the ten-string model was the most common. Some examples apparently included an optional endpin to support this behemoth on the floor. Despite some poetic hype in Gibson's 1912 catalog, suggesting that the harp guitar was as superior to the regular guitar as the piano is to the harpsichord, the cumbersome and expensive Style U (costing around $400) never became very popular. Its most prominent role today is as a conversation piece hanging on the walls of numerous guitar shops.

HARP GUITAR

(Symphony model, style 8)
Made by Larson Brothers for distribution by W. H. Dyer & Brother
United States (Chicago, Illinois), about 1920

CHRIS KNUTSEN of Port Townsend, Washington, first patented a
harp guitar of this style in 1898. But after his patent expired in 1912,
the Larson Brothers of Chicago were asked to produce a similar
model for distribution by W. H. Dyer & Brother at their music store
in St. Paul, Minnesota. With a large, sweeping arm terminating in
a mushroom-shaped headstock to carry the bass strings, this is one
of the most stylish designs for a harp guitar. The long extension of
the body adds more than just visual interest and structural support,
however. Covered by the same resonant spruce wood as the rest of
the top, this additional portion of the hollow "sound box" imparts a
deep, reverberant quality to the instrument's tone. In consequence,
players generally favor the sound of this style of harp guitar over
others. This particular harp guitar was the fanciest of the Larson/
Dyer line at the time, with pearl binding around the body and
soundholes, and pearl fingerboard inlay in a "tree-of-life" pattern.

83

HARP GUITAR

Harmony Company
United States (Chicago, Illinois), about 1920s

PROBABLY NO OTHER INSTRUMENT is more qualified for the title "bizarre guitar" than this one. And yet some creative person working in the shop of Chicago's Harmony Company is known to have made at least two and possibly three of these twin-bodied instruments. On most harp guitars the long bass strings run to a second set of tuners mounted on a structure added to the main headstock or body. But here the strings are carried to a second guitar body seamlessly fused to the other. The result is an undulating piece of

musical and sculptural fantasy. One of the previous owners of this exceptional contraption was a naturalist and storyteller named Sam Campbell, who, while working in public relations for the Chicago and Northwestern Railroad, used the instrument to accompany himself in songs that encouraged travelers to visit the Great Northwest. Friends of the guitar's current owner have in turn suggested many amusing names for the instrument, including the Push-Me-Pull-You, Straddlevarius, Stereosaurus, and Goitar.

GUITAR-LYRE
Luigi Mozzani (1869–1943)
Italy (Cento), about 1910

BORN IN THE northern Italian town of Faenza, Luigi Mozzani began guitar studies at a young age at the music conservatory in nearby Bologna. A versatile musician, he worked as an oboist for a time in the 1890s before turning seriously to the classical guitar. Dissatisfied with the small parlor-type guitars that were common in Italy at the time, Mozzani, like many musicians before him, began designing his own instruments. He not only learned the craft of guitar making but established schools of lutherie in Bologna, Cento, and Roverto. His most brilliant pupil was Mario Maccaferri (1900–1993), a promising guitarist who likewise took an interest in building instruments and went on to create his own highly original guitar designs. During thirteen years of working with Mozzani, Maccaferri helped him in the construction of several magnificent guitars like this one, which Mozzani called a *chittara-lyra* (guitar-lyre). This instrument reflects the Art Nouveau style of the early twentieth century, with organic, curvilinear shapes derived from nature. One of the more interesting technical features of Mozzani's harp guitars is a bolt-on neck, the angle of which can easily be adjusted.

Flat-top Guitars

UNTIL THE LATE NINETEENTH CENTURY, virtually all guitars were made with flat tops. But with the introduction of other varieties of guitars in the twentieth century, like arch tops, resonator guitars, and, ultimately, electric instruments, the term "flat-top guitar" became necessary to differentiate this basically traditional form from the newcomers. More specifically, the designation "flat-top guitar" came to mean an instrument that used steel strings, whereas the older type outfitted with gut strings came to be called the classical guitar.

From the early 1900s until the 1940s, manufacture of steel-strung flat-top guitars flourished, as numerous companies produced a wide variety of instruments in all price ranges. Chicago was an especially large center of instrument manufacture, home to Lyon and Healy, Harmony, Stromberg-Voisinet, and Larson Brothers. But the long-established firms of Gibson in Kalamazoo, Michigan, and C. F. Martin and Company in Nazareth, Pennsylvania, led the field in terms of design and quality. Martin is credited with many improvements in flat-top guitar construction, especially with a pattern of crossed wood struts called X-bracing that supports the top, which the company had already developed by the 1850s. Yet Martin was also surprisingly conservative, waiting until the 1920s to issue their first guitar specifically designed for steel strings. Big companies such as Lyon and Healy may have sold more instruments, but far more Martin and Gibson guitars from this period survive today.

Played with picks of tortoiseshell, plastic, or metal, steel-strung guitars are considerably louder than gut-strung instruments played with bare fingertips or nails, and as such, they lend themselves to a quite different style of playing. The rise of the flat-top guitar in the early twentieth century paralleled the evolution of many forms of popular music, especially vocal-based genres such as folk, country, and blues, all of which were well suited to the twangy yet agreeable accompaniment of steel strings. The flat-top guitar was an ideal tool for music of the people, portable enough to make an appearance at picnics, dances, and back porches, and versatile enough to provide music from church to barroom. And the price was right, too; a basic guitar could still be bought for less than five dollars in the 1940s.

FLAT-TOP GUITAR

(D-45 model)
C. F. Martin and Company
United States (Nazareth, Pennsylvania), 1938

MARTIN'S DREADNOUGHT MODEL has met with more success and been copied more often than any other acoustic guitar of the twentieth century. Designated by the letter D, this wide-bodied instrument was named after the largest class of English battleships from the early 1900s. Martin first produced large guitars like this in 1916, although they were for sale only through the Ditson Company, based in Boston and New York City. But in 1931, as players increasingly sought more volume from guitars, Martin made the first Dreadnoughts for distribution under their own name. The number 45 in the model's name denotes Martin's fanciest style, which incorporates a border of abalone and ivory-grained celluloid binding around the top, back, and soundhole. Compared with many of the presentation-style instruments sold by firms such as Lyon and Healy earlier in the century, the D-45 may seem plain. The Martin Company traditionally limited the decoration on their guitars, instead focusing on superior construction and tone quality. The first D-45 was made in 1933 on special order for cowboy star Gene Autry, and only ninety more were made before 1942. The few surviving pre-war D-45s are now among the world's most valuable guitars in the vintage market.

A guitar sounds good even if you drop it on the floor. A beginner can find music in the guitar that has escaped the virtuoso. It's a magical instrument, constrained by a short range and a peculiar tuning, that produces music beyond the limits of its own nature.
— LEO KOTTKE

FLAT-TOP GUITAR
(SJ-200 model)
Gibson, Inc.
United States (Kalamazoo, Michigan), 1938

AS THE COUNTRY'S foremost maker of arch-top guitars, Gibson resisted making flat-top models until 1926. But not long after C. F. Martin added the big Dreadnought guitar to its line of instruments in 1931, Gibson countered with its own similarly shaped Jumbo model. Then, late in 1937, Gibson introduced a distinctly different large guitar called the SJ-200 (for Super Jumbo), with a wide, almost circular lower bout and a narrow waist reminiscent of nineteenth-century German guitars. The first SJ-200 was made for cowboy film star Ray Whitley, composer of "Back in the Saddle Again." Whitley was looking for a guitar with an especially powerful bass sound to accompany his vocals. For a guitar made at the end of the Great Depression (and retailing at $200), the SJ-200 had very deluxe appointments, with gold-plated hardware, crest-shaped pearl fret markers, multilayered edge binding, a bridge shaped like a handlebar moustache (or maybe steer horns), and a pick guard adorned with flowering vines. It was just the thing to make a performer stand out, whether on stage or screen. Ninety-six SJ-200s were made before World War II, after which the model was renamed simply the J-200.

*A different guitar will have different strengths and weaknesses.
If you learn how different guitars want to be touched, you have
a wider repertoire of tonal technique on all guitars. My guitars
were frequently my teachers.*

— DAVID BROMBERG

FLAT-TOP GUITAR
Larson Brothers (Prairie State brand)
United States (Chicago, Illinois), about 1935

WITH A TWENTY-ONE-INCH-WIDE body, this abnormally huge
guitar was probably a custom order. It achieves its aim of increased
volume, but the girth is more than many players can easily handle,
and the exaggerated proportions are a little freakish for most tastes.
If nothing else, it demonstrates the upper limits of what can be
done with the guitar shape. Carl and August Larson were among
America's most prolific and talented makers of guitars and mandolins during the early twentieth century, though virtually all of their
products were distributed under brand names other than Larson,
including Stahl, Dyer, Maurer, Euphonon, and Prairie State. These
two unassuming brothers from Sweden were among the first to
create flat-top guitars specifically for use with steel strings, and examples made under their Prairie State brand featured two internal
steel rods that braced the body and neck. With metal resisting much
of the string tension, the wood parts could be made thinner and
lighter, leading to a generally bright tone and a reduction of weight
even in large instruments like this brute.

BELL-SHAPED GUITAR
(5270 model)
Lyon and Healy (Washburn brand)
United States (Chicago, Illinois), about 1925–29

CHICAGO'S LYON AND HEALY COMPANY was known for offering guitars with ornate inlay and binding under the Washburn brand name. Their bell-shaped model, produced between about 1925 and 1929, shows that they also tried to entice customers with a nontraditional shape. The form may have been suggested by one of the many European craftsmen working in the Washburn shop familiar with the cittern, a smaller wire-strung instrument sometimes made in bell shape by eighteenth-century German makers. The gold foliate pattern decal on the top is also rather antique in conception, reminiscent of stencil-work decoration on American furniture from the 1830s. Lyon and Healy claimed to be striving for a different tonal character with the bell-shaped guitar, and advertised that at $165 it was for "the player who feels that he must have the very best guitar that money can buy." One noted owner was American author Carl Sandburg, who supposedly once used his bell-shaped Washburn to serenade Marilyn Monroe.

FLAT-TOP GUITAR

(Rhumba model)
The Fred Gretsch Company, Inc.
United States (Brooklyn, New York), about 1933–35

THE IDEA OF MAKING a circular guitar has occurred to more
than one instrument maker over the years. Such well-known builders as Panormo and Lacôte built oval-shaped guitars during the
nineteenth century. With their Rhumba model, the Gretsch Company may have been trying to attract guitar players who wanted the
look of a banjo, if not the sound. During the 1920s the tenor banjo,
with its four metal strings and louder sound, was more popular than
the guitar because it could compete with wind instruments used in
the dance and jazz bands of the era. Its association with the tango
dance craze of the 1910s sometimes gave it the name "tango banjo."
Gretsch probably hoped to capitalize on the popularity of another
Latin dance fad by naming their round, banjo-shaped guitar the
Rhumba model. By the time it was introduced, though, guitars were
becoming louder and beginning to usurp the banjo's dominance.
Whatever tonal attributes the Gretsch Rhumba possessed, its production was short-lived, as devoted guitar players were not attracted
to such a nontraditional shape.

COWBOY GUITAR
("Singing Cowboys" model)
Harmony Company
United States (Chicago, Illinois), 1942

I once played a guitar that a friend bought for $20, and I thought, "Wow, I can finally play standards on this thing!" The guitar was practically a toy—which forced a certain economy of approach—but I loved its sound and cheapness. There was a certain paradoxical relationship between constraint and freedom that was brought out by this crappy guitar.

— MARC RIBOT

WITH THE ADVENT of singing cowboys in films of the 1930s, everyone wanted to strum along to "Home, Home on the Range." The result was a market for inexpensive guitars stenciled with folksy western scenes, many depicting stars such as Roy Rogers and the Lone Ranger. The Harmony Company's "Singing Cowboys" model is typical of the genre, with a simple, monochromatic scheme: a group of cowpokes gathered around the campfire after a long day on the trail, conjuring up a more romantic life than any real cattle drover would attest to. Owned by Sears, Roebuck and Company after 1916, Harmony produced more than half the guitars of all types made in the United States by the early 1940s. But they specialized in mid-priced to low-end instruments, some of which, like cowboy guitars, seem remarkably cheap now (this particular model cost $4.45). Present-day collectors covet these kitschy instruments far more for their nostalgic value than for their tone quality.

Arch-top Guitars

ORVILLE H. GIBSON, an inventive instrument maker working in Kalamazoo, Michigan, was the first to produce a line of guitars and mandolins made with tops and backs carved with an arch, as on a violin. The group of businessmen who bought Gibson's fledgling enterprise in 1902 adopted few of his quirky notions about the actual construction of "arch-top" instruments. But the general idea of arch-top guitars would prove to be the one on which the Gibson Company would build its reputation, creating some of the industry's most influential designs. By the 1930s, several other manufacturers had begun trying to capture some of Gibson's share of the arch-top market, resulting in a competitive flourish during the next three decades that brought forth some guitars of remarkable style, beauty, and tone.

Following World War I, people were ready for a more exciting and cosmopolitan style of music than the kind played by the mandolin orchestras that had dominated the entertainment scene at the turn of the century. The new form that grabbed everyone's attention was jazz, featuring boisterous wind instruments such as trumpets and saxophones. At first, the only string instrument that could compete in this new cacophony was the tenor banjo, but instrument makers quickly rose to the challenge of making a louder guitar that could handle the job. With a relatively large body carrying heavy-gauge metal strings to provide maximum volume, arch-top guitars with their punchy sound soon became a regular fixture in jazz ensembles and dance bands. Guitarists initially limited themselves to playing chords as part of a band's rhythm section, and most seemed reluctant to step beyond this role. But electronic amplification and a hot young player named Charlie Christian soon demonstrated that the guitar could ably pluck out a solo line as well.

Constructing an arch-top guitar is no easy matter, as considerable skill is required to shape the top and back into a form that is both aesthetically pleasing and acoustically dynamic. As a result, the finest arch-top guitars were quite expensive when new, and individually crafted examples by masters such as Stromberg and D'Angelico still command remarkably high prices. Befitting their role in jazz music, many classic arch tops exhibit the kind of flashy styling that was previously reserved only for tenor banjos. Use of patterned celluloid plastic for bindings, pickguards, and headstock decoration became especially prevalent, as it created a luxurious look without expensive natural materials such as pearl, ivory, and tortoiseshell. Much more so than before, both large companies and smaller independent makers also began to prominently display their name on the headstock, creating brand-name recognition.

The guitar has a far greater repertoire—and a far greater adaptability to the music that's happening everywhere around you—than any other instrument. Whether it's adapting film music, or playing jazz, pop, or rock, the guitar belongs there in spirit. It's not out of its depth, and the repertoire is absolutely incredible and never-ending.

—JOHN WILLIAMS

ARCH-TOP GUITAR
(L-5 Master Model)
Gibson, Inc.
United States (Kalamazoo, Michigan), 1924

THE INTRODUCTION OF Gibson's L-5 model was a landmark in guitar history. With its handsome "Cremona brown" finish and two F-shaped soundholes like those on a violin, rather than a circular or oval opening, the L-5 became the basis for virtually all successful arch-top designs that followed. It was originally intended as part of a group of four so-called Master Model instruments, the other three of which were different-sized mandolins. The creator of this line was Lloyd Loar (1886–1943), an accomplished musician who came to Gibson in 1919 and assumed the role of acoustic engineer. Loar personally executed the most critical steps of construction for every Master Model instrument: tuning, carving, and tonally adjusting the top, back, and interior braces. He then signed his work, but it is thought that only fifteen to thirty L-5 guitars were made between 1922 and 1924 with his seal of approval. The fashion for mandolin orchestras had faded by the 1920s, but guitarist Eddie Lang soon adopted an L-5 for his seminal jazz performances, and Maybelle Carter used one to pluck out distinctive bass runs in the early country sound of her family trio.

ELECTRIC ARCH-TOP GUITAR
(ES-150 model)
   Gibson, Inc.
      United States (Kalamazoo, Michigan), 1936

DEBUTING LATE IN 1936, the ES-150 was the first commercially successful electric guitar made with a regular or "Spanish" neck rather than one set up to be played Hawaiian-style—that is, with a steel bar held in the left hand. It was called an "Electro-Spanish" (ES) model and retailed for $150, including a critical accessory, an amplifier. Equipped with this cutting-edge instrument, jazz great Charlie Christian made history as the first prominent electric guitarist, trading riffs with clarinetist Benny Goodman in his popular big band starting in 1939. As is often the case with new technologies, many potential users were slow to come around, so the market among jazz performers for unamplified arch-top guitars continued well into the 1950s, despite the proven success of instruments like the ES-150. As popular music of the twentieth century got louder and louder, though, virtually every guitarist eventually had to get plugged in. This very early ES-150 belongs to rock-blues-jazz guitarist J. Geils, who played it for certain cuts on his album *Blues Time*.

For me, the guitar played without a pick becomes a more expressive instrument.
— CHARLIE BYRD

ARCH-TOP GUITAR
(Orchestre model)
Designed by Mario Maccaferri for Selmer & Cie
France (Paris), 1932

FEW JUXTAPOSITIONS OF GUITARIST and guitar maker are more celebrated than Django Reinhardt (1910–1953) and Mario Maccaferri (1900–1993), yet strangely, the two men never met. Reinhardt was a Gypsy performer whose hot jazz style inspired generations of players. Maccaferri was a successful guitarist in the classical style, but was equally talented at instrument making. In the early 1930s, the Selmer Company had Maccaferri design a series of guitars, including the Orchestre model, which players also called the Jazz model. The body had a flat cutaway on the treble side for better access to high notes, and a large D-shaped soundhole, making it an easily recognized instrument. The internal construction was equally unusual, with a special resonating chamber and reflector added to boost volume. Although acoustically practicable, the complex arrangement of these interior structures and their tendency to come loose caused many owners to have them removed. The Orchestre model was discontinued after only about one hundred were made, and Maccaferri left Selmer in 1933, not entirely amicably. Selmer soon introduced another guitar of the same shape, but with a smaller oval soundhole and no internal resonator. Reinhardt played both models, his name ultimately becoming much more associated with the design than either Maccaferri's or Selmer's.

ARCH-TOP GUITAR

(Venetian model, style A)

Kay Musical Instrument Company (Kay-Kraft Brand)

United States (Chicago, Illinois), about 1933

KAY MUSICAL INSTRUMENTS was one of numerous Chicago companies churning out guitars in the first half of the twentieth century, having evolved about 1931 from the Stromberg-Voisinet firm. Joseph Zorzi (1878–1977), an Italian-born violin maker, was in charge of Kay's arch-top guitar production. He had worked twenty-nine years for crosstown rivals Lyon and Healy, at times adding fancy inlay to their Washburn-brand presentation guitars. Zorzi helped develop a nontraditional guitar model for Kay, featuring two asymmetrical points projecting from the upper half of the body. Kay's owners were supposedly not enthusiastic about this so-called Venetian shape at first, but it eventually won enough approval to go into production. The guitar was offered in mahogany, maple, or rosewood, denoted as styles A, B, and C, respectively. The gilt foliate decal on the body and molded plastic facing on the headstock aspire to high style, but like most Kay instruments the Venetian model was a moderately priced guitar, with top and back bent (rather than hand carved) to a slight arch. An interesting technical feature is that the neck angle is adjustable by loosening a small bolt at the heel, although this requires an awkward reach through the soundhole.

101

Arch-top guitar

(Airway W4 model)
Willi Wilkanowski (1886–about 1960)
United States (Brooklyn, New York), 1938

SEVERAL NINETEENTH-CENTURY luthiers made violins in guitar shape, so it was inevitable that someone would create a guitar that looked like a violin. An arch-top guitar was especially appropriate since the violin had inspired its design to begin with. Polish-born violin maker Willi Wilkanowski may not have been the first to make a guitar with pointed corners like a violin, but his work is probably the best known. He came to America about 1920 and, after working for the Ditson Company in Boston and Gretsch in New York, eventually set up his own shop in Brooklyn. It is said that he made over 5,000 violins during his long career but only about thirty arch-top guitars, all constructed between 1938 and 1941. This particular guitar is one of Wilkanowski's fanciest, with wide chunks of abalone shell outlining the body and pickguard. Of special note is the highly figured back carved from a single plank of maple, stock that may have originally been procured to make cellos. Wilkanowski's arch tops are undeniably arresting, but they were a bit too eccentric to attract any particularly well-known players. Thirty years later, the Hofner Company in Germany manufactured a line of bass guitars with a small violin-shaped body, made popular by Paul McCartney during his years with the Beatles.

ARCH-TOP GUITAR
(Super 400 model)
Gibson, Inc.
United States (Kalamazoo, Michigan), 1934

JUST AS GIBSON'S L-5 arch-top guitar, introduced in the mid-1920s, quickly became a model everyone else copied, so too did their Super 400 model after it debuted in 1934. With an eighteen-inch-wide body, enormous headstock, and engraved metal tailpiece, it was bigger and better than any other arch top of the time. Fancy "split-block" pearl fret markers, luxurious seven-layer binding around the body, and an ornate marbleized pickguard all combined to make an exceptionally stylish instrument, a fact recognized even by non-guitar players. The Super 400 created a new benchmark for what an arch-top guitar could look like, stimulating the imaginations of other guitar makers for years to come, both in large companies and in small shops. Priced at $400 (and given its model number to match), this extravagant guitar flew in the face of the Great Depression and its financial straits. But the over-the-top appearance served to boost Gibson's reputation as the premier maker of high-end arch-top guitars, while the oversized body supplied the volume needed to cut through the big band sound of the jazz era. This particular Super 400 is one of the very first made, bearing the name "Muzzy" on the headstock for its original owner, jazz guitarist Muzzy Marcelino.

ARCH-TOP GUITAR
(Synchromatic 300 model)
The Fred Gretsch Company, Inc.
United States (Brooklyn, New York), about 1946–49

MANY BRANDS OF arch-top guitars from the 1940s and 1950s showed great flair in their design, but those made by the Gretsch Company were especially artistic. Introduced the same year as the 1939 World's Fair in New York, the Synchromatic model exemplified a new style called "Streamline Moderne," characterized by curvilinear shapes suggesting motion and fluidity. This aesthetic is most evident in the Synchromatic's elongated teardrop soundholes and the undulating outline of the light bulb–shaped headstock. Punctuating the effect are hump-shaped fret markers, thirteen plies of black and white plastic binding, and boisterous tortoiseshell-figured bands along the sides of the body and fingerboard. The stair-stepped pattern incorporated into Gretsch's "chromatic" tailpiece, "synchrosonic" bridge, and Grover-brand tuning machines is clearly derived from another prevalent style of the 1930s, Art Deco. A clear or natural finish was first offered on arch-top guitars in 1939. Present-day collectors have generally favored these rarer light-colored instruments over those with the more common shaded brown finish.

ARCH-TOP GUITAR
(New Yorker model)
John D'Angelico (1905–1964)
United States (New York, New York), 1954

JOHN D'ANGELICO is regarded by many to have been America's most gifted guitar maker, and his instruments are among the most admired and highly sought by players and collectors alike. After an apprenticeship that began at age nine with a grand-uncle, in 1932 he opened his own shop to build guitars, mandolins, and violins. D'Angelico's earliest arch tops are modeled after Gibson's successful L-5 model, but he kept abreast of the market, soon adding larger models with seventeen- and eighteen-inch-wide bodies. No mere copyist, D'Angelico created a distinctive look for his top-quality instruments, adding geometric decoration inspired by the outlines of skyscrapers that graced his Manhattan skyline. This New Yorker model is an example of his fanciest and biggest guitar, with a cutaway on the treble side of the body. Like most quality arch tops of the period, the back is made of robustly striped maple, enhanced on this instrument by a shaded "sunburst" finish that vaguely emulates the wear on old violins. D'Angelico continued to appoint his New Yorker guitars in the Art Deco fashion until his death, but by the 1950s such styling was long out of date, just as the jazz age that created a desire for big arch-top guitars was fast fading.

Hawaiian, Resonator, and Lap Steel Guitars

HAWAIIAN MUSIC WAS REMARKABLY POPULAR everywhere during the first half of the twentieth century. Stylistically it was based on the guitar, which had been introduced to the islands by nineteenth-century Portuguese, Hispanic, and American settlers. Hawaiian-style guitar playing has two unique aspects: first, the instrument's body is laid flat across the lap; and second, rather than using the fingers of the left hand to press the metal strings against the fingerboard, the player grasps a small steel bar and glides it along their surface, hence the oft-used term "steel guitar." The resulting sound is fluid and lilting, invoking an idyllic land of soft ocean breezes and swaying palm trees.

Playing guitar with "slide steel" technique was already well established in Hawaii by the turn of the twentieth century, and the fashion was gradually disseminated abroad. But exposure to the alluring sounds of island music escalated tremendously in 1915, as an estimated 17 million visitors attended the Panama-Pacific International Exposition in San Francisco. One of the most popular attractions at the event was an elaborate and expensive pavilion sponsored by the Hawaiian Chamber of Commerce, complete with hula dancing and live music played on guitars and their smaller cousins, ukuleles. As a result, thousands rushed to buy such instruments and emulate the melodious sounds.

Hawaiian music did not have a tremendous effect on other musical styles, but its popularity and performance method gave rise to some interesting and important steps in the evolution of the guitar. Early blues guitarists adopted the slide technique for their distinctive songs, although how that tradition developed remains a bit uncertain. For generations, guitar makers and players had also sought more volume from their instrument, and the steel strings and hollow necks used on Hawaiian guitars provided a bit of increased projection. But more sophisticated attempts at making a louder instrument arrived during

the 1920s in the form of the resonator guitar. These peculiar instruments use shallow discs of spun aluminum rather than a wood top to amplify sound. The Slovakian-born Dopyera family, working in Los Angeles, was especially successful in the development of "resophonic" guitars. Louder than traditional instruments of the time, resonator guitars also have a distinctly bright tone. Most early resonators were made with square-shaped necks for Hawaiian-style playing, but some were also constructed with a regular rounded or "Spanish" neck that was favored by performers of blues, country, and folk music.

For a brief time, resonator instruments were at the forefront of guitar technology, but it was not long before electrically amplified instruments took their place. So-called lap steels were the first commercially successful electric guitars, and as evidenced by the large number of surviving examples from the 1930s through the 1950s, they once had a tremendous following. The limited number of guitarists who play lap steels today (apart from those who play their evolutionary descendant, the pedal steel) places them in a category that some feel is outside the true domain of the guitar. It would be a mistake to dismiss their influence on the instrument's history, though, as they paved the way for the acceptance of electric guitars. Lap steels exhibit some of the most imaginative designs of any musical instrument of the twentieth century. As they were relatively straightforward to construct and not bound by any previous traditions, their designers made abundant use of new materials, exciting colors, and marvelous shapes.

HAWAIIAN STEEL GUITAR
(style 4)
Hermann C. Weissenborn (1863–1937)
United States (Los Angeles, California), mid-1920s

AS INTEREST IN HAWAIIAN guitar playing grew during the 1920s, a German-born instrument maker named Hermann Weissenborn became the leading American maker of Hawaiian-style steel guitars. The beautifully figured koa wood he used for his instruments is native to Hawaii, and has long been used there for making guitars and ukuleles. Weissenborn guitars were made in four styles, each with increasing amounts of rope-pattern binding; the "style 4" was the most expensive at $79, with binding along every edge of the body, neck, and soundhole. The sloping shoulders and square hollow neck present no interference to the player because both hands approach the strings from above, as the instrument is held flat across the lap. Astoundingly light and resonant, Weissenborn instruments produce a tone with such a long sustain that it seems to take forever to completely fade away. Hawaiian music has never made a serious comeback since its decline in the 1950s, but modern performers such as David Lindley and Ben Harper have championed Weissenborn instruments with eclectic musical styles that incorporate imaginative ideas about slide guitar playing.

GUITAR

(catalog model 49)
Stromberg-Voisinet Company
United States (Chicago, Illinois), about 1932

AS MORE AND MORE mainlanders visited the Hawaiian Islands in the early twentieth century, scenes inspired by the tropical paradise were applied to every conceivable article, from ashtrays to shirts. Given the guitar's central role in Hawaiian music, and its large flat surface that invites ornamentation, it was only a matter of time before palm trees and sunset beaches made their appearance on inexpensive instruments like this one. Despite the picturesque setting depicted on its top, this guitar is not set up for Hawaiian-style playing, lacking a raised nut to lift the strings high off the surface of the fingerboard. Stromberg-Voisinet (later the Kay Company) was one of several large Chicago firms that produced all sorts of musical instruments, but was not related to the guitar-making Stromberg family in Boston. Most of their guitars were in the low-to-mid price range; this catalog model 49, with Hawaiian scene as a standard feature, was probably sold through the Chicago Musical Instrument Company for about $15. The mottled celluloid plastic applied to the headstock, fingerboard, and pickguard is sometimes referred to by the period trade name "pearloid," though many modern-day collectors affectionately call such materials "mother-of-toilet-seat."

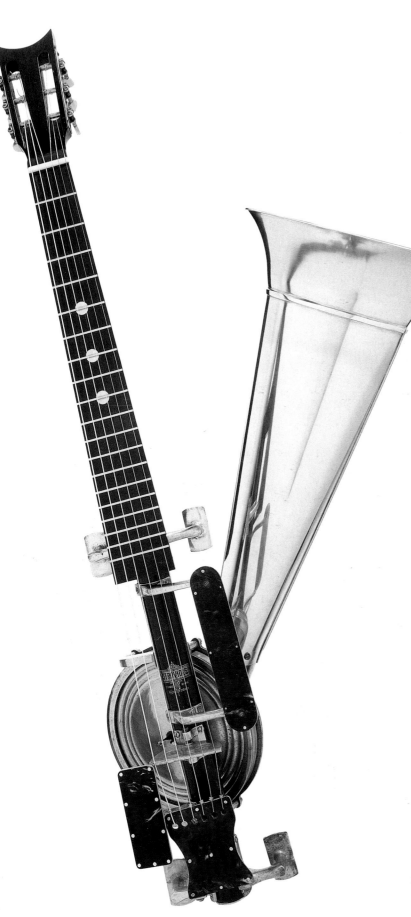

STROH GUITAR

(Hawaiian model)
> Probably by George Evans and Company
> England (London), about 1920

AT FIRST GLANCE, this guitar looks like something inspired by the outlandish inventions of Rube Goldberg or the books of Dr. Seuss. But it was intended as a serious instrument. John Matthias Augustus Stroh (1828–1914), a German-born inventor working in London, was granted a patent in 1900 for a violin that uses an aluminum diaphragm and horn rather than a hollow wood body to amplify its sound. Given the primitive state of audio recording at the time, these instruments were found to work better in the studio than their traditional counterparts because they were louder and their sound was more directional. After 1909, George Evans and Company succeeded Stroh's son Charles in the manufacture of Stroh instruments, and introduced guitars, mandolins, ukuleles, and banjos to the line. Although inelegant and mechanical-looking to modern eyes, the curious appearance of the Stroh guitar seems somehow appropriate to an era when other inventions like the phonograph and motorcar also proudly displayed their horns.

RESONATOR GUITAR

(Tri-cone model)
> National String Instrument Corporation
> United States (Los Angeles, California), 1934

FIRST MANUFACTURED IN 1927, the Tri-cone is the earliest of various designs for a resonator guitar created by performer George Beauchamp and inventor John Dopyera (1893–1988). As the name implies, the Tri-cone employs three shallow aluminum cones (covered by grillwork in the lower half of the body) to amplify the sound of the strings, which are acoustically coupled to the cones by a T-shaped bridge. The Tri-cone also has a hollow neck for added resonance, a feature Dopyera may have adopted from the Hawaiian-style guitars made by neighboring craftsman Hermann Weissenborn. At least as radical as the Tri-cone's acoustical structures are its body and neck of nickel alloy covered with shiny nickel-silver plating. The gleaming metallic finish and geometric latticework are distinctly in the Art Deco style, but this "Machine Age" look is oddly juxtaposed with delicate engraved flowers on the front, back, and sides that are much more Victorian in flavor.

The first time I played "Praise God I Am Satisfied" by Blind Willie Johnson, it made me sick, so I put some Bill Monroe on the phonograph. But that sound kept coming back to me—five minutes later, I had to hear Blind Willie again. I listened to it again and started crying. I thought it was the most beautiful thing I had ever heard.

—JOHN FAHEY

RESONATOR GUITAR
(model 65 prototype)
Dobro Company
United States (Los Angeles, California), 1929

NOT LONG AFTER producing the first resonator guitars under the brand name "National," factory superintendent John Dopyera became dissatisfied with his partner's management of the firm and left to start his own company with his brothers Rudy and Emil. To compete against the Tri-cone model he had patented for National, Dopyera developed a cheaper resonator guitar with one large cone for amplification. This new model was manufactured under the name "Dobro," an abbreviation of "Dopyera brothers." Early Dobros had wood bodies and aluminum resonators, though some later models had metal bodies as well. The scrolling pattern sandblasted into the body of this prototype instrument is reminiscent of European folk art, perhaps harking back to the Dopyera family's Slovakian origins. To the uninitiated, the perforated "pie-plate" cover on a Dobro seems rather mysterious, appearing to hide something a bit too mechanical for a string instrument. Indeed, some traditional guitar companies of the time dismissed Dobros and other resonator guitars as gimmicks rather than "real guitars." But the twang and wail of the Dobro appealed to many blues and country musicians, its unique sound complementing their own plaintive singing style.

114

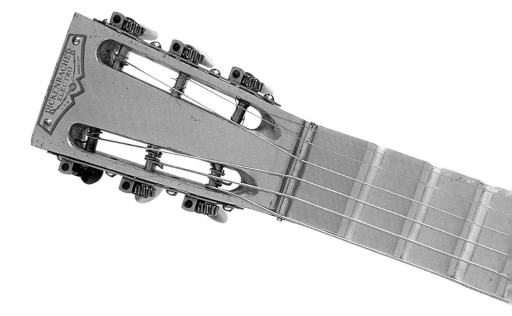

LAP STEEL GUITAR
(A-22 model)
Electro String Instrument Corporation (Rickenbacker brand)
United States (Los Angeles, California), 1934

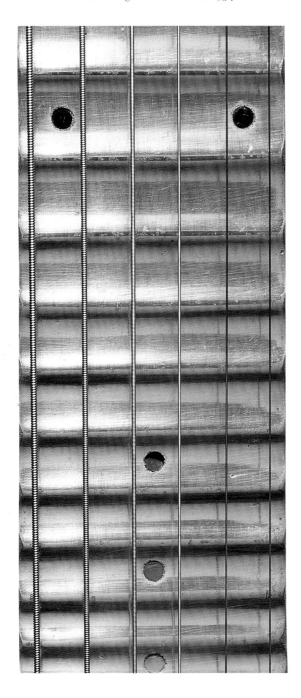

ALTHOUGH QUIRKY LOOKING, the Rickenbacker A-22 lap steel is one of the twentieth century's most important musical instruments. Nicknamed the "Frying Pan," it was the first commercially successful electric guitar, though designed to be laid flat across the lap for Hawaiian-style playing. There had certainly been earlier experiments with electrically amplified guitars, but none that were perfected or that went into major production. The A-22 was developed by performer/inventor George Beauchamp and others in conjunction with Adolph Rickenbacker (1892–1976), who had come to Los Angeles from Switzerland in 1918 and set up a shop for metal stamping in 1925. By 1928 Rickenbacker was making metal parts for resonator guitars built by the National String Instrument Company. Given Rickenbacker's background in metalworking, it was logical that the company chose aluminum for their first instrument. Yet the Frying Pan's unassuming and nontraditional form also follows the functional use of metal in Bauhaus-style furniture from the mid-1920s. One reason that the Electro String Instrument Corporation succeeded with these early electric guitars where others had failed was their use of a superior pickup that transferred string vibrations electromagnetically rather than with a cruder microphonic system. The A-22 (whose model number designates its 22-inch string length) first went into production in 1932, and versions were still offered as late as 1958.

LAP STEEL GUITAR

(BD model)

Electro String Instrument Corporation (Rickenbacker brand)
United States (Los Angeles, California), about 1950

THE SECOND GENERATION of Rickenbacker-brand lap steel guitars, introduced in 1935, had bodies molded into diminutive guitar
shapes using Bakelite plastic. Bakelite is less reactive to temperature
changes than the aluminum the company had used earlier for its
"Frying Pan" lap steels, but it is also heavier. To keep weight down
in the new B model, the dense plastic body was hollowed out in
certain areas and the openings disguised by slightly domed plates
that were chromed in some versions and painted white or black in
others. Use of Bakelite also allowed the frets to be molded as part
of the fingerboard, just as those on the Frying Pan were cast into
the upper surface of its metal neck. In 1949, a slightly more deluxe
Rickenbacker BD model was added to the line, shown here in a
seven-string version.

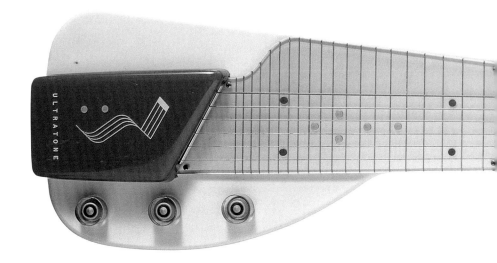

LAP STEEL GUITAR
(Dynamic model)
Valco (National brand)
United States (Chicago, Illinois), 1952

IN SPITE OF NUMEROUS business restructurings experienced by
the companies that used the National brand name, their instruments
consistently showed an imaginative approach to styling, beginning
with the first resonator guitars of dazzling nickel silver introduced
in the late 1920s. National lap steels from later decades were no
exception, exhibiting astute awareness of design trends that influenced the look of other traditionally style-conscious products, such
as radios and automobiles. The Dynamic model lap steel is a marvelous example of Valco's flair for design, resulting in an intrinsi-
cally engaging object regardless of whether one is interested in its
ability to produce sound. The black and white color scheme creates
a clean, elegant style, and the curved shapes of the headstock, body,
and control knob plates all suggest the streamlined look that was
still prevalent when the Dynamic was first introduced in the 1940s.
The pattern of stepped fret markers owes more to the slightly older
fashion of Art Deco, while the colored geometric shapes punctuate
the instrument with a playful, graphic element.

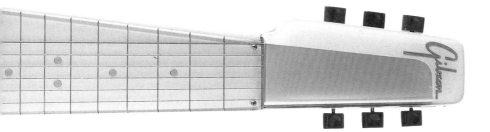

LAP STEEL GUITAR

(Ultratone model)
Gibson, Inc.
United States (Kalamazoo, Michigan), about 1949

AFTER WORLD WAR II, Gibson and many other guitar manufacturers were sure that interest in Hawaiian music and the lap steels used to perform it would continue with the same vigor as during the 1930s. So in 1946 Gibson confidently launched their high-style Ultratone model, and featured it on the cover of their first postwar catalog in 1949. Gibson enlisted the aid of the industrial design firm Barnes and Reinecke in Chicago to create the sleek, streamlined body of the Ultratone, whose styling is not unlike household appliances of the time. Although the body is of wood, its rounded corners imitate the look of molded plastic, while the soft ivory finish is complemented by bright coral tuning knobs and pickup cover to create an especially harmonious color scheme. During its years of production, the Ultratone was offered in various decorator colors, including salmon and deep blue. The postwar period saw a declining interest in the carefree sound of Hawaiian music, as more vigorous genres like jazz and eventually rock and roll took its place. No amount of good looks could save the Ultratone and other lap steels from losing out to regular electric guitars, which were quickly becoming perfected and were certainly more versatile.

THE 1950s

UNLIKE ANY PRIOR TIME, the 1950s saw vast numbers of teenagers with
money in their pockets, ready to spend it on whatever caught their fancy—like
the latest hit record. Music has always been a powerful tool for self-expression,
and a wild new form called rock and roll gave the country's youth an especially
effective means of rebelling against their parents. The key sound in this music,
considered by many to be morally dangerous and excessively loud, was the
electric guitar.

The designers of the first successful solid-body electric guitars in the 1950s
could never have imagined what icons of pop culture their instruments would
eventually become. After all, the Fender Company's now classic Telecaster and
Stratocaster instruments were initially developed for southern Californian players of country swing, who dominated the live music scene at the time. Likewise,
the enduring Les Paul model developed by Gibson was endorsed by a performer
whose best-known tune was the Hit Parade favorite "How High the Moon." In
fifty years, the shapes of these instruments have undergone virtually no change
by their manufacturers, and are still among the best-selling and most copied
styles of electric guitar. Even to those who do not know what they are called,
the "Strat" and "Les Paul" have become two of the most recognizable symbols
of popular music.

The electric guitar has mainly been associated with males, so it is no
surprise that beginning in the postwar era, designers of guitars have frequently
drawn inspiration from cars for both shape and finish. Since solid-body guitars
use electronic pickups rather than a hollow resonating chamber to amplify
their sound, these instruments are not bound to any particular shape, allowing
makers to freely explore forms from curvy to angular. The designs for early
electric guitars now seem tentative compared to the many novel models introduced in decades since. It is a fact, though, that much of the fundamental
problem-solving in making a good electric guitar was worked out a half-century
ago, and many models from the drawing boards of the '50s are still in production. Likewise, players and aficionados have come to venerate the surviving
instruments from this golden decade of electric guitar design, creating an active
market for modern copies and, regrettably, forgeries.

ELECTRIC GUITAR
(Telecaster model)
> Fender Electric Instrument Company
> > United States (Fullerton, California), 1957

THE WORLD'S FIRST mass-produced solid-body guitar, the Fender
Telecaster has been in continuous production longer than any other
instrument of its kind. Its inventor, Leo Fender (1909–1991), set
out to create an electric guitar without the feedback caused by the
hollow body of earlier types. He first introduced his idea in 1950
with the Fender Esquire, using one electric pickup, followed a few
months later by a two-pickup version called the Broadcaster. The
latter's name was changed a year later to avoid infringement on
another company's line of drums. "Telecaster" was chosen to suggest cutting-edge technology, like the new term "television." By
today's aesthetic standards, the squarish body of the "Tele" seems
clunky, and was criticized by some as a slab of wood that anyone
could cut out with a bandsaw. But this was the genius of Fender's
concept, simplifying construction to first principles. Equally innovative was the solid maple neck bolted to the body, allowing easy
replacement. A dark walnut "skunk stripe" down the back conceals
a metal truss rod that allows adjustment of the neck. The frets are
set directly into the neck's upper surface, eliminating the need for
a separate fingerboard. This 1957 Telecaster has a cloudy blond
finish reminiscent of Danish Modern furniture, but Fender also
began to offer instruments in bright lacquer colors made by Dupont.
The Telecaster was initially targeted toward guitarists playing western swing, but was soon adopted for all types of popular music.

124

PAIR OF ELECTRIC GUITARS

(Stratocaster model)
Fender Electric Instrument Company
United States (Fullerton, California), 1963 and 1964

AT FIRST GLANCE, the Stratocaster guitar might appear to be simply a refinement of the shape Fender had worked out for the Telecaster model a few years earlier. But a second look reveals a far more sensuous figure, with contours not unlike a curvaceous sports car. The edges are all gently rounded and the upper rim beveled to allow a comfortable fit against the player's body. Like the Telecaster, the "Strat" has remained largely unchanged and uninterrupted in production since the first examples finished in a traditional brown sunburst left the factory in 1954. Fender further exploited the automotive aesthetic by offering instruments in solid colors like the "Sonic Blue" and "Fiesta Red" seen on this pair from the early '60s. Arguably the world's most recognizable electric guitar, the Stratocaster has been copied in varying degrees by countless other makers. Some suspect that Fender himself borrowed the design of

I've always liked the Freddie King/B. B. King rich tone, and at the same time, I like the manic Buddy Guy/Otis Rush Strat tone. So I'm always caught in the middle of the Gibson and Fender sounds. If I'm playing my black [Fender] Strat, and I'm in the middle of a blues, I kind of wish I was playing a [Gibson] Les Paul. Then again, if I was playing a Les Paul, the sound would be great, but I'd be saying, "Man, I wish I had the Stratocaster neck!"
— ERIC CLAPTON

the sideways-scroll headstock (seen in slimmer form on the Tele-caster) from guitars made in the late 1940s by Paul Bigsby. The same shape, however, had been used throughout the nineteenth century by Austrian and German guitar makers. The Stratocaster has become a timeless design in its own right, with its unmistakable "horns" projecting from the body. Its most important technical feature was a built-in tremolo system (now usually called a whammy bar) that allows the player to musically "bend" notes by releasing tension on all the strings. The Stratocaster has been the guitar of choice for countless musicians, including Buddy Holly, Eric Clapton, and Jimi Hendrix.

Early on, I figured out that when the top of a guitar is vibrating and a string is vibrating, you've got a conflict. One of them has got to stop, and it can't be the string, because that's making the sound. So in 1934, I asked the Larson Brothers—Chicago instrument makers—to build me a guitar with a half-inch-thick maple top and no f-holes. They thought I was crazy.

— LES PAUL

ELECTRIC GUITAR
(Les Paul model)
Gibson, Inc.
United States (Kalamazoo, Michigan), possibly late 1950s

BY THE 1950S, the Gibson Company had enjoyed decades of dominance in the arch-top guitar market, and had also achieved considerable success with their first flat-tops in the late 1930s. But the arrival and acceptance of Fender's solid-body Telecaster caught them unprepared. Guitarist and recording studio wizard Les Paul had previously approached Gibson with his own ideas about electric guitars, and was laughed at when he showed them a homemade but highly functional instrument he called "The Log." But by 1952 the public's interest in solid-body electric guitars could no longer be ignored, and Gibson began distributing its Les Paul model, now willing to cash in on the name of the popular performer. Paul's actual role in the design of the guitar that bears his name has often been disputed, but the instrument has served a myriad of players over the past half-century, and the eighty-five-year-old Paul continues to play one at a weekly gig in New York City. This particular guitar is one of many still owned by Les Paul, which, like every instrument that belongs to the inveterate tinkerer, has had its electronics amended and customized repeatedly.

ELECTRIC GUITAR

(Les Paul model)
Gibson, Inc.
United States (Kalamazoo, Michigan), 1952

WHEN THE FIRST Les Paul models were being prepared for launch into the solid-body guitar market in 1952, Gibson was looking for some way to make a big impression. Les Paul himself suggested that they issue the instrument in a luxurious gold-colored finish, a decorative scheme that was retained for the next six years. Called "gold tops" in the vintage guitar trade, some instruments were in fact colored gold on the sides and back as well. The solid-color paint masks the underlying structure, composed of a mahogany body with a carved three-piece cap of maple, theoretically resulting in a guitar that combines the tone of these two woods. Compared with Fender's Telecaster and Stratocaster models, the perfectly rounded outline of the Les Paul (reminiscent of certain Gibson arch tops) is anything but radical. It is also a heavy guitar, but in compensation for the load it puts on the guitarist's back it has a tone that players find extremely versatile. The earliest Les Pauls featured a wire-like string holder called a "trapeze" tailpiece, combined with the bridge. Players were not enthusiastic about this design, since it interfered when trying to dampen the strings with the palm of the hand.

ELECTRIC GUITAR

(Roundup 6130 model)
The Fred Gretsch Company, Inc.
United States (Brooklyn, New York), 1955

WITH ITS ROUNDUP MODEL, the Gretsch Company was apparently making a serious attempt to appeal to the sensibilities of country guitarists by appointing the instrument with stereotypical "western" motifs on almost every conceivable part. There are longhorns and cacti engraved on the fret markers, a big metal belt buckle on the tailpiece, tooled leather with metal studs around the edges of the body, and a top veneered with knotty pine and the letter G (for Gretsch) branded into it. In the 1950s, country performers were among the most avid users of electric guitars. Solid-body instruments were most popular in the music scene in southern California, whereas Nashville artists generally preferred hollow-body models. Gretsch never captured a share of the guitar market to equal Gibson's or Fender's, but no one denies that when it came to eye-catching instruments they were number one.

133

ELECTRIC GUITAR

(Flying V model)
Gibson, Inc.
United States (Kalamazoo, Michigan), 1958

IN THE POSTWAR PROSPERITY of the '50s, industrial designers sought a modern look in everything from toasters to teacups, and guitars were not immune to this trend. Gibson president Ted McCarty (born 1909) designed a trio of futuristic guitars to appeal to younger players, who were typically opting for his competitor's products. The instruments were to be made out of African limba, an excellent tone wood that Gibson marketed as Korina. Only two models of the "Korina Trio" (Flying V, Explorer, and Moderne) went into production in 1958, and those in very limited numbers. The Moderne (looking like an asymmetrical Flying V with one short leg) was apparently never produced. Whether it was the space race or the fins on a Cadillac that inspired the creation of the Flying V (pronounced vee), its aeronautic shape and pointed headstock definitely suggested motion and excitement. Dealers loved having them on display, but the radical new look was just too bizarre for most players, and many went unsold, leading Gibson to discontinue the model after two years. Bluesmen Albert King and Lonnie Mack adopted the Vee into their musical arsenals, but the peculiar shape ultimately appealed mainly to rock guitarists of the 1970s and '80s, resulting in many reissues of the model by Gibson and countless copies by others. Far from ergonomic, the balance of the Flying V feels strange, and the sloping lower edge readily slides off a seated player's knee, causing some examples to be outfitted with a corrugated rubber pad on this surface.

135

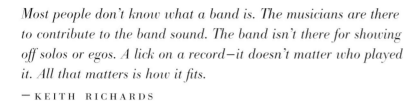

Most people don't know what a band is. The musicians are there to contribute to the band sound. The band isn't there for showing off solos or egos. A lick on a record—it doesn't matter who played it. All that matters is how it fits.

— KEITH RICHARDS

ELECTRIC GUITAR

(Explorer model)
Gibson, Inc.
United States (Kalamazoo, Michigan), 1963

THE EXPLORER GUITAR shares the angular lines of its sister model, the Flying V, but with its in-cut sides it might be seen as a cubist interpretation of the traditional guitar's figure-eight shape. To complement this off-kilter form, the headstock is also angled, in what is sometimes called a scimitar shape. Both the Explorer and the Flying V made a big splash in the musical instrument industry when they were unveiled, shaking up notions of what direction guitar styling could take. But neither model sold very well, and fewer than two dozen Explorers are believed to have left the factory in the late 1950s. Although datable to 1963 by its serial number, this particular Explorer was constructed from parts left over from the original production batches of 1958 and 1959. The Explorer's design is now considered a classic, rather than the startling ultramodern experiment it set out to be. Gibson began reissuing the Explorer model in 1975, and its retro space-age look has become especially popular among hard-rock guitarists.

137

ELECTRIC GUITAR

(White Falcon 6136 model)
The Fred Gretsch Company, Inc.
United States (Brooklyn, New York), 1956

GIBSON AND FENDER had more initial success with their electric guitars than the Gretsch Company, but they were never as adventurous in their color schemes and decorative details. Gretsch set out to top the look of all its competitors when it introduced the prototype of its White Falcon model at a trade show in 1954. Retailing at a whopping $600 (the most expensive guitar of the Gretsch line), it sported a creamy white finish set off by gold sparkle binding and gold-plated hardware. The jazzy-looking tailpiece drew inspiration from the Cadillac logo, and a V-shaped notch in the top of the headstock mirrored its energetic style, while wings inlaid below it and engraved into the pearl fret markers emphasized the avian name. Gretsch boasted that "cost was never considered in the planning of this guitar." Despite great styling and a trendy name, the White Falcon never became strongly identified with any particular guitarist, but Falcons have been played by both Neil Young and Brian Setzer.

ELECTRIC GUITAR
(6120 model)
The Fred Gretsch Company, Inc.
United States (Brooklyn, New York), 1955

IN 1954, THE GRETSCH COMPANY scored a coup by signing on noted country and jazz guitarist Chet Atkins to endorse their guitars and offer advice about design. Over the next two decades, Gretsch created a number of hollow- and solid-body electrics with Atkins's help, though he was always known for playing the former. Starting in the mid-1950s, the Gretsch Company made a conscious effort to produce guitars with flamboyant styling, and they were the first to offer instruments in lively colors, like the amber red of this 6120 model. Some of the first Atkins "signature" guitars were decorated with overt western motifs, including the "G" boldly branded into the top, but the cowboy look died down by the early 1960s. According to its famous owner, this is only the second 6120 from the Gretsch factory, a guitar that Atkins's fans associate with an important period in his long and successful career. Atkins is most discriminating when it comes to tone, so the electronics of this guitar have been custom wired to his specifications. Early rockers Eddie Cochran and Duane Eddy also played Gretsch 6120s, but with a considerably different technique than the stylish finger-picker who is often called the "Country Gentleman."

ELECTRIC GUITAR

(ES-335 model)
Gibson, Inc.
United States (Kalamazoo, Michigan), 1958

I didn't know anything about style when I started. I mean, I knew what a style was, but I wasn't aware of having one myself. That sort of thinking was far too technical for me at that time. But putting a song together—now that did come in anticipation of a melody I heard in my head, or by jamming with someone, or hearing something somebody else was doing and thinking I might like it to go a little differently. But I still do not recognize any style of my own.

— CHUCK BERRY

ONE OF GIBSON'S best-selling guitars since its introduction in 1958, the ES-335 model was created to fuse the company's tradition of great hollow-body guitars with the advantages of a solid-body instrument. The result was a guitar that appears to be all hollow, but in fact has a four-inch-wide bar of solid maple down the center of the inside, reducing some of the screeching feedback that amplified hollow bodies are prone to when played at high volume. As a result, the ES-335 (ES meaning "Electric Spanish") is equally at home in mellow jazz and boisterous rock and roll. With a thin profile and weighing only seven and a half pounds (a Les Paul model can weigh as much as twelve), it also provides a physically comfortable alternative to big-bodied arch tops and heavier solid bodies. The dual cutaways at the top of the body result in a look guitarists call "Mickey Mouse ears," but offer easy access to the highest notes on the fingerboard. Rock and roll pioneer Chuck Berry played the ES-335, and blues legend B. B. King has also long been associated with guitars of this type. Gibson's current "Lucille" model (the name King has given to every guitar he owned) is made without soundholes, supposedly to further reduce feedback, but King had already solved this problem early on by stuffing paper in the holes.

THE 1960s

AMONG ITS MANY LEGACIES, the 1960s will long be remembered as a decade that spawned astonishing creativity in popular music. In the course of a short ten years, rock music was radically transformed from a primitive, three-chord genre to an incredibly rich and innovative medium, encompassing styles as diverse as the well-orchestrated sound of the Beatles and the thrashing chords of hard-rock groups like the Who. At the center of much of this artistic expression was the guitar, usually featured in the fairly standard makeup of a rock band: drums, bass, and two electric guitars playing the roles of rhythm and lead.

There were no radical developments in the actual construction of guitars during the '60s, but a number of means evolved for making electric instruments more expressive. As amplifiers became more powerful, rock guitarists cranked up the volume and discovered how to use electronic feedback and distortion to expand their musical palette. Some of the first separate electronic "effects" were also invented, with names like "fuzz tone" and "crybaby wah," that allowed the guitar to produce strange, psychedelic sounds. And the era gave rise to rock music's first "guitar gods," with stage personas that were larger than life and solo performances that were at times excessively longwinded.

Although guitars of the '60s were made using existing technology, manufacturers still introduced new shapes and finishes that they hoped would appeal to buyers. But as none of the new designs could compete with the performers' onstage outfits, many musicians such as Jimi Hendrix, George Harrison, and Eric Clapton had instruments personalized with wild designs painted in Day-Glo colors. As the visibility of pop music idols increased, so did their awareness of the image they projected in public. With this in mind, some players began choosing their guitars not only for their sound quality but also for their visual appeal, as the "axe" increasingly began to take on the role of a large piece of jewelry hanging around the neck.

ELECTRIC GUITAR
(Les Paul/SG Standard model)
Gibson, Inc.
United States (Kalamazoo, Michigan), 1961

GIBSON'S FIRST SOLID-BODY electric guitar, the Les Paul, was a big success in the early 1950s, but its sales slacked off by the end of the decade. The proposed solution was to aggressively restyle the design into one that departed from the original's traditional shape. Debuting in 1961, the new model featured a thin, symmetrical body of lightweight mahogany with heavily beveled edges and two barb-like points at the upper end, creating a "bat-wing" effect. With the fingerboard joining the body at the highest fret, the neck takes on an extra-long appearance, while offering players easy access to the highest notes. The automotive-styled chrome hardware, coupled with a deep red finish, gave the instrument a very luxurious look. This was the first Gibson guitar with a vibrato unit as standard equipment, although it was a side-pull system that didn't work especially well. Les Paul's main complaint, however, was the overall body design, so after his endorsement agreement with Gibson ended in 1963, the company renamed this guitar model the SG (for solid guitar). Famous players of the SG include Jerry Garcia of the Grateful Dead and Eric Clapton during his years with Cream.

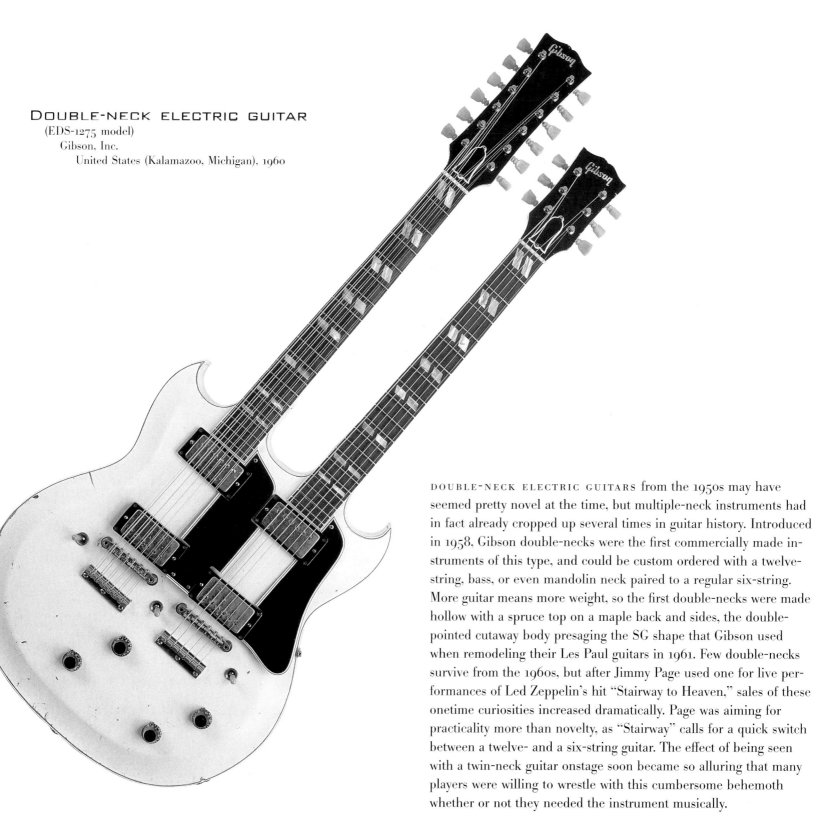

DOUBLE-NECK ELECTRIC GUITAR

(EDS-1275 model)
Gibson, Inc.
United States (Kalamazoo, Michigan), 1960

DOUBLE-NECK ELECTRIC GUITARS from the 1950s may have seemed pretty novel at the time, but multiple-neck instruments had in fact already cropped up several times in guitar history. Introduced in 1958, Gibson double-necks were the first commercially made instruments of this type, and could be custom ordered with a twelve-string, bass, or even mandolin neck paired to a regular six-string. More guitar means more weight, so the first double-necks were made hollow with a spruce top on a maple back and sides, the double-pointed cutaway body presaging the SG shape that Gibson used when remodeling their Les Paul guitars in 1961. Few double-necks survive from the 1960s, but after Jimmy Page used one for live performances of Led Zeppelin's hit "Stairway to Heaven," sales of these onetime curiosities increased dramatically. Page was aiming for practicality more than novelty, as "Stairway" calls for a quick switch between a twelve- and a six-string guitar. The effect of being seen with a twin-neck guitar onstage soon became so alluring that many players were willing to wrestle with this cumbersome behemoth whether or not they needed the instrument musically.

ELECTRIC GUITAR

(360-12 model)
Electro String Instrument Corporation (Rickenbacker brand)
United States (Los Angeles, California), 1966

A FEW TWELVE-STRING acoustic guitars were built in the early 1900s, and one made by the Stella Company was made famous by the legendary blues singer Lead Belly. Major companies like Martin and Gibson first offered acoustic twelve-strings in the 1960s, but the Rickenbacker 360-12 was the first truly successful electric model. In 1964 one of the prototypes for this instrument was presented to George Harrison of the Beatles, who can be seen and heard playing it in the film *A Hard Day's Night*. Soon afterward, Roger McGuinn of the Byrds bought a 360-12 and made its jangling, chiming tone part of his band's signature sound in tunes like "Mr. Tambourine Man." Unlike twelve-string guitars of other types, the Rickenbacker reverses the order of the octave strings on the lowest four courses, placing the low or fundamental note first when strumming downward. To make tuning easier and alleviate crowding on the headstock, the twelve tuning pegs are ingeniously staggered at right angles.

ELECTRIC GUITAR

(Mk VI model)
Vox Company
England and Italy, late 1960s

DESPITE GIVING BIRTH to some of the most famous rock bands of the 1960s, England produced no guitar companies that could successfully compete with America's. One problem was the failure of British firms to use sales literature to promote their instruments as aggressively and with the same sense of sex appeal as their overseas counterparts. Vox guitars were made in England between 1961 and 1964, after which time production was moved to Italy until the early 1970s. They were one of the only homegrown manufacturers from the United Kingdom to achieve much success, but as with other English guitar companies, their products were more popular domestically than abroad. The Mk VI, nicknamed the "Teardrop," was one of the most unconventional guitar styles of its time, with a simple egg-shaped body and matching headstock outline. The model got considerable exposure in the hands of Rolling Stones guitarist Brian Jones, who played a rare two-pickup version of the Mk VI finished in white. But even being seen on *The Ed Sullivan Show* was not enough to create a strong demand for this or any other Vox model.

I look for a deep, gutty feelin' in a guitar tone. I don't use picks. People ask, "How you get that?" It's just there. There's a lot of people try to play real fast chords—da da da da da—that ain't the hard, solid blues. It's synthetic. It has no feeling to it. You sit down and play some funky, funky guitar. Take your time! Don't rush it. Just let it come flowing through you. I can play guitar so funky, it'll bring teardrops to your eyes.

—JOHN LEE HOOKER

ELECTRIC GUITAR

(3012 model)
Danelectro Corporation
United States (Neptune City, New Jersey), about 1960

GUITARS DESIGNED BY Nathan Daniel (1912–1994) never reached the pantheon of instruments made by Fender, Gibson, and Martin. But in their own way they were no less influential, their low price tag making them readily available to the masses. Daniel designed a line of budget electric guitars, first distributed in 1954 by Sears, Roebuck and Company under the Silvertone brand, which many famous players fondly remember as their first guitar (especially a model that came with an amplifier built into the case). In 1956, Daniel began retailing guitars under his own Danelectro brand, creating some thoroughly original models over the next dozen years that collectors now cherish because of their "cheap but cool" aesthetic. Cost cutting was achieved through materials and construction. As with this 3012 "short horn" model in "bronze" finish, the top and back of many Danelectro instruments were made from one-eighth-inch Masonite glued over a poplar framework, and covered over with a painted finish (including trendy colors like fuchsia and peach). The most distinctive feature of "Danos" is their single-coil electronic pickups made from actual chromed lipstick tubes that were purchased from a cosmetics manufacturer. In recent years, Danelectro guitars have begun to be manufactured again, with the same appearance but better-quality materials, for players seeking both a retro look and a retro tone.

I got fed up with Fenders because they were too clean, but I liked them because they were tough. The Fender would last two or three shows—and ten minutes if I wanted to smash it up.

— PETE TOWNSHEND

Oh it breaks my heart to see those stars
Smashing a perfectly good guitar

— JOHN HIATT

ELECTRIC GUITAR

(Telecaster Pink Paisley model)
Fender Musical Instruments
United States (Fullerton, California), 1969

THERE ARE FEW IMAGES that conjure up the late 1960s like a paisley pattern in hot pink. It may seem strange that Fender opted to apply such an unconventional look to its traditionally functional Telecaster guitar rather than to its decidedly hipper Stratocaster model, but the flat shape of the "Tele" actually lent itself much better to this surface treatment. To achieve it, Fender simply purchased an adhesive-backed foil wallpaper printed with the paisley pattern (along with one in a foppish blue "flower power" design) from the Borden Chemical Company of Columbus, Ohio. Both of these psychedelic fashion statements were dropped about a year after their first appearance in 1968, as the fad for paisleys and big flowers died out faster than Nehru jackets and love beads. Strangely enough, the one noted guitarist who played a Pink Paisley Telecaster was James Burton, one of Elvis Presley's band members. Burton was initially concerned about what Presley might think of this odd-looking guitar, but he claims that the King loved it.

ELECTRIC GUITAR

(Bianka model)
Hoyer Guitars
Germany (Tennenlohe), 1961

KIDS IN POSTWAR EUROPE were as hungry for pop music as the youth of America, and their link to it was often through the U.S. troops stationed there. But getting hold of guitars to emulate their rock, jazz, and country idols was no easy task. American guitars were costly to import, and few European firms produced instruments of comparable quality. Hoyer Guitars, based in the town of Tennenlohe (just north of Nuremberg), was one of the first major German companies to make electric instruments. Their Bianka model is a revealing example of how other countries sometimes interpreted the visual elements of a modern guitar, invoking aesthetic values quite different from those of American companies. For unknown reasons, the maker has carved both the spruce top and the maple back of the Bianka guitar in a pattern of ridges, creating an exciting texture on what is normally a flat surface. More striking in a literal sense are the soundholes, outrageously shaped like lightning bolts, while the kaleidoscopic pattern of the extremely wide plastic binding adds a further burst of outlandish flavor. European guitar firms eventually began to style their guitars much more closely after classic American instruments, but one can only wonder what marvelous styling might have been lost as a result.

New Materials

MOST OF THE WORLD'S MUSICAL INSTRUMENTS are made primarily of wood, a versatile, abundant, and (most importantly) resonant material. While the makers of quality string instruments put much effort into selecting appropriate stock, they have also had to recognize that wood, an organic material, varies greatly from piece to piece in density and grain structure. When synthetic materials with a more uniform structure began to appear in the twentieth century, it was inevitable that experimenters would explore their usefulness for making musical instruments.

After World War II, plastics became one of the predominant materials for fabricating objects, valued both for their ability to mold into almost any shape and take on almost any color, and for a dizzying array of chemical formulations, each possessing different characteristics of flexibility and durability. Few would argue that synthetic materials possess the same warmth of tone found in a piece of fine-quality spruce, but experimentation with these substances has sometimes resulted in guitars that sound surprisingly good.

Despite its seemingly intractable nature and cold feeling, even metal has been fashioned into string instruments. The flexible properties of aluminum were put to innovative use as early as the 1920s in the amplifying cones of resonator guitars, whose nickel silver and brass bodies were equally radical for the time. Certain makers of solid-body electric guitars have been attracted to metal as well, especially for making necks, where the material's rigidity helps maintain stability and create a sustained tone.

Neither instrument makers nor consumers have yet shown any genuine willingness to stop using wood for most of the guitars currently being made, however. It will be interesting to see if the new century produces any significant change of attitude or construction methods, especially as supplies of traditional guitar woods are becoming increasingly scarce.

Guitar

(Romancer model)

Mastro Industries

Designed by Mario Maccaferri (1900–1993)

United States (New York, New York), about 1960

MARIO MACCAFERRI was a guitarist and instrument designer who immigrated to the United States in 1939 after working on guitar models used by legendary jazz performer Django Reinhardt. Following up on some success in developing plastic reeds for woodwind instruments, Maccaferri introduced a line of incredibly popular plastic ukuleles in 1949 (supposedly over nine million were sold in twenty years), succeeded by several models of plastic guitars beginning in 1953. Some of these instruments were intended for young beginners and the toy market, but the full-size models were meant to be legitimate yet affordable guitars, and they sound remarkably good. Made from Dow styrene, only some of Maccaferri's plastic guitars had pictorial decoration. The Romancer model is certainly the most amusing, graphically depicting just how popular you could be if you played a guitar in the 1950s. There are girls in poodle skirts, hit 45s spinning on the record player, and teens everywhere smiling. And check out that guy in the cardigan sweater on the headstock; he and his guitar are getting quite the admiring looks from those three young ladies.

157

ELECTRIC GUITAR

(Glenwood 99 model)
Valco (National brand)
United States (Chicago, Illinois), 1963–64

ONE OF THE MOST original designs produced by the always stylish Valco company was a group of guitars first sold in 1962, whose "map-shaped" outline vaguely resembled the United States (though probably not intentionally). A few of these models were made with a solid wood body, but the more interesting ones were constructed of "Res-O-Glas," a recently developed type of plastic made from a two-part resin with glass fibers added to the mix. Designed for speedy and cost-effective production, the body was formed from two molded halves of this fiberglass material encased over a narrow wood core. The seam was then joined with a flexible strip of vinyl. Vibrant colors like the sea-foam green of this instrument were added directly into the resin mixture, allowing a depth of color and iridescence not possible with painted-on finishes. The Glenwood 99 was the fanciest of Valco's map-shaped guitars, with its "butterfly" inlays on the fingerboard. Although some collectors now consider these colorful National-brand guitars the quintessential "cheap and cool" instrument, they were not all that inexpensive when new, and they never caught on with any major performers. The design was discontinued after only three years, and the Valco company itself did not last much longer.

158

ELECTRIC GUITAR

(7000 4V model)
Oliviero Pigini and Company (EKO brand)
Italy (Recanati), early 1960s

IN THE EARLY 1960s, Tom and Guy LoDuca ran a thriving musical instrument company in Milwaukee that specialized in accordions. As the market for "squeeze boxes" declined, the LoDuca brothers quickly turned their business efforts toward increasingly popular guitars, which they distributed under the brand name of EKO. Teaming up with Oliviero Pigini, one of their former accordion suppliers in Italy, they were able to boast a number of different guitar models by 1964. EKO guitars were relatively inexpensive, and their primary market was novices rather than professionals. Pigini's factory had manufactured accordion bodies using plastic that could be heat-molded around tight curves and into various shapes. The earliest EKO electrics were made with this same versatile material, available in a dazzling array of sparkle and simulated pearl finishes, many with contrasting fronts and backs. All in all, the attractive shape of this EKO guitar shows the excellent sense of line, form, and innovative use of plastics that distinguished Italian design in the 1960s.

BORN IN THE SMALL TOWN of Cavriago in north-central Italy, Wandré Pioli is unquestionably one of the most eccentric guitar designers of recent times. Greatly influenced by Milanese artistic currents of the previous century, he refers to himself as the last of the *scapigliati*, an artist of life. Pioli's creative expression has ranged from decorating vehicles to designing leather clothing, but in the late 1950s he was drawn to guitar manufacture and constructed an unconventional circular-shaped factory in his hometown for this purpose. Pioli designed and produced many unusual guitars through the mid-1960s, some of which are now specifically sought out as *objets d'art*. All are unconventional in some way, and the most extreme border on bizarre. This Karak model is representative; its wide, organic shape of bright blue plastic laminate shows a typically Italian concern for form. Particularly unusual is the way the aluminum alloy neck (sheathed in plastic) pierces the concave body as a one-piece structure from headstock to bridge. Except for the Davoli-brand pickups, all the fittings are custom designed, from the quirky concave tuning knobs to the W-shaped whammy bar assembly. The mottled green laminate covering the sides is equally funky, finished with chrome edging reminiscent of kitchen tabletops of the period. It is, altogether, a truly distinctive guitar that borrows virtually none of its elements from American instruments of the time.

ELECTRIC GUITAR
(Karak model)
Wandré Pioli (born 1926)
Italy (Cavriago), about 1965

ELECTRIC GUITAR
(Dan Armstrong model)
Ampeg Company
United States (Linden, New Jersey), 1969–70

STARTING IN THE 1960s, various mechanical objects were made from clear plastic to show their inner workings, including radios, clocks, and telephones. Musical instruments were a logical choice for this treatment too, and some drums, pianos, and guitars got the see-through look. The Fender Company produced a one-of-a-kind Stratocaster electric guitar entirely out of clear Lucite plastic in 1964 to illustrate every aspect of the instrument's construction. But it was respected guitar designer and repairer Dan Armstrong who designed this clear plastic instrument to be manufactured by Ampeg, a company best known for its amplifiers. Although labeled as the Dan Armstrong model, players simply referred to it as the "See-through," a name Ampeg supposedly later trademarked. The maple neck and rosewood fingerboard may have made the instrument feel more natural to players, but like the faux rosewood pickguard and headstock they hinder the guitar from fully exploiting its transparent look. A unique technical feature of this guitar is the single-coil electronic pickup designed by Bill Lawrence, which can easily be changed for one with different specifications by sliding it out of a wide slot cut into the body.

ELECTRIC GUITAR

(Veleno Original model)
John Veleno (born 1934)
United States (St. Petersburg, Florida), 1974

MANY GUITAR BUILDERS have used aluminum for their instruments' necks because it is rigid and lightweight, but machinist John Veleno was inspired to build an all-aluminum instrument after constructing a guitar-shaped mailbox of the same material to advertise his sideline as a guitar teacher. The body is constructed in two halves carved from solid blocks of aluminum and plated with a mirror-like chrome finish. The black-colored neck is cast from a composite of aluminum and magnesium, with the fingerboard as an integral part of the unit. The body shape is fairly traditional, although the V-shaped headstock exhibits a personal, if not entirely successful, flair for design. Aluminum is not as susceptible to humidity changes as wood, but some players find the feeling a bit too cold. Veleno is thought to have made about 185 instruments before ceasing production in 1977. During that time several famous guitarists purchased and played Veleno instruments, including Eric Clapton, Gregg Allman, Lou Reed, and Mark Farmer of Grand Funk Railroad.

The extreme dynamic and percussive possibilities of an acoustic guitar amplified through a bridge pickup have, over many years of performing, informed not only the way I play, but the way I write and sing too. My guitar taught me to sing in textures, from the roundest lingering harmonic to the sharpest snap of a pulled string. Being a percussion instrument as well as a melodic instrument, my guitar also teaches me about the relationship between rhythm and melody. Portable. Did I mention it also taught me about being portable?

— ANI DIFRANCO

ACOUSTIC/ELECTRIC GUITAR

(Adamas model)
Ovation Instruments Division of Kaman Music Corp.
United States (New Hartford, Connecticut), 1981

ELECTRIC GUITAR

(Electraglide model)
Andrew Bond
Scotland (near Inverness), 1985

NO OTHER PRODUCTION GUITAR of the twentieth century has a more recognizable appearance than one developed by Charles H. Kaman (born 1919), a guitar lover and engineer who had founded an aircraft company. In 1966, Kaman's newly formed Ovation Company introduced a guitar with a one-piece bowl-shaped back made of molded fiberglass. When they first appeared, Kaman's guitars were too radical for conservative-minded players, but in 1969, singer/guitarist Glen Campbell appeared playing an Ovation on his weekly TV show, giving a huge boost to the instrument's visibility and acceptance. The first Ovation models had a traditional spruce top, as do many of the guitars they still make. However, the top of the Adamas model, introduced in 1976, is composed of a thin, 1/32-inch core of birch wood, sandwiched between even thinner layers of carbon graphite fibers. The small soundholes at the upper end of the body eliminate the need for a large hole cut out of the middle. The use of space-age materials and a bright red top on this early Adamas cutaway model are oddly contrasted with the carved foliate headstock and multi-wood epaulette around the soundholes, reflecting the craft-revival look popular during the 1970s.

FOR HIS ELECTRAGLIDE GUITAR, Scottish guitar maker Andrew Bond adopted graphite fiber to create a smart and elegant instrument with a one-piece body and neck. Its design reflects the "black-box" look that prevailed in countless appliances during the 1980s, in which control knobs were blended in with the body and an all-black color scheme was combined with clean lines to create a sophisticated, high-tech appearance. The Electraglide evinces that modernistic aesthetic with push-button controls (rather than knobs) and a digital LED readout, while the fingerboard with its sawtooth pattern of stepped and slanted planes rather than traditional frets is equally unconventional. Introduced in 1984, the Electraglide was designed in conjunction with David Stewart of Eurythmics. U2 guitarist the Edge also endorsed Bond's instrument and made a considerable financial investment in the venture. But difficulties in manufacture and a comparatively high retail price kept sales of this handsome graphite guitar low, ultimately causing production to cease by 1986.

THE 1970s

MUSICALLY SPEAKING, THE 1960s were a hard act to follow. That decade
had been so extraordinarily fertile from an artistic standpoint that its effects
still resound throughout much of popular music. But the music scene of the
early '70s began on uncertain footing, as the Beatles disbanded and the lives
of several prominent rock stars, among them Jimi Hendrix, were cut tragically
short. In their place were many eminently forgettable groups catering to the
teenybopper crowd and the rise of an insipid form of dance music called
disco, causing some music historians to wish that the 1970s could have been
skipped altogether.

The guitar's musical landscape was not entirely barren during this period,
however. Heavy-metal rock began to flourish, especially under the influence of
the group Led Zeppelin, whose guitarist, Jimmy Page, extended the sonic palette of the electric instrument with audacious ideas, such as using a violin bow
to excite the strings. Other musical forms employing the electric guitar also
began to appear during the '70s, such as fusion, which combined elements of
jazz with rock, and funk, which gave a uniquely African-American sound to
pop music. A new generation of pop-folk singers such as Joni Mitchell, John
Denver, and James Taylor revived the steel-string acoustic guitar, while others
countered with the raw electric sound of a raucous genre called punk rock.

Within the field of industrial design, the guitar has often suffered from
excessive conformity, and the guitar-buying public largely ignored the few
innovations in the visual and technological features of the instrument during
the 1970s. Players had become quite comfortable with two fundamental models of electric guitar, the Stratocaster and the Les Paul, and were reluctant to
consider much that strayed too far from these norms. The Fender and Gibson
companies, which had created these instruments twenty years earlier, were
unsuccessful in introducing new designs, and there arose a worldwide industry
in copying at least the shapes of these two successful models, if not always their
essential principles. Other guitar makers who attempted to initiate new styles
faced considerable bias as well in this conservative climate. In the spirit of hot-
rod owners, some guitarists began to customize off-the-shelf instruments with
improved electronic components and other hardware, always in search of the
perfect musical machine.

*I don't use effects. I tried a wah-wah pedal once.
Stubbed my toe on it. Forget it!*

— CHUCK BERRY

ELECTRIC GUITAR

(331 model)

Electro String Instrument Company (Rickenbacker brand)
United States (Los Angeles, California), 1971

IN THE LATE 1960S you could buy stereo speakers with built-in colored lights that flashed in response to the music, allowing any owner to create a kaleidoscopic nightclub show right at home. The idea was likewise used in electronic organs, but Rickenbacker reasoned that such a gimmicky light show could also be easily adapted to an electric guitar by concealing small colored lights in the body beneath panels of frosted plastic. As with the speakers, the lights in the Rickenbacker 331 model flashed in response to different pitches played on the guitar. A separate transformer was used to supply electricity to the lights, but the arrangement is said to have been prone to overheating. Although this guitar seems best suited to bands clinging to the psychedelic fad of the previous decade, it was country guitarist Buck Owens who most often showed off the instrument on the corny television show *Hee Haw*. Like most fads, the light-show guitar was quite short lived, and was manufactured only between 1970 and 1975.

ELECTRIC GUITAR

(IC300 Artist Iceman)
Ibanez Company
Japan, 1978

JAPANESE MUSICAL INSTRUMENT companies began making solid-body electric guitars not long after they were first launched in America in the early 1950s. Much of their effort has been applied toward copying successful American products, notably the Strato-caster, the Les Paul, and other classic models. Ibanez began making guitars in 1962, and during much of the 1970s did well in exporting good imitations of American brands (so good, in fact, that the company eventually ended up in court in a patent infringement case). For Japanese customers, however, Ibanez concurrently produced imaginative shapes such as the Iceman, which they eventually marketed abroad, giving them original-looking models in their export line. The form of the Iceman is hard to categorize, but the comma-like hook on the treble side is the most distinctive feature. The outline is probably most recognizable to rock audiences as the basis for a guitar played by Paul Stanley of Kiss, who had one made with small pieces of mirrored glass glued to its top to appear as if it had been shattered.

ELECTRIC GUITAR

(Flyte model)
Burns UK Ltd.
England (London), about 1976

DURING THE 1970S, English guitar makers had no better success competing with their American counterparts than they had in the previous decade. But there were a few talented individuals striving to be recognized, including Jim Burns (1925–1998), who is sometimes called the British answer to Leo Fender. Despite certain quirks in their designs, Burns's guitars were generally superior in construction to those made by U.K. competitors Vox and Watkins, and they had gained some cachet through their endorsement by the band the Shadows, popular in England during the early '60s. In 1965 the factory that Burns had started was bought by the Baldwin Piano and Organ Company. Baldwin ceased making guitars by 1970, but production of Burns guitars was resumed under new ownership from 1974 to 1977 with several odd-looking electric instruments like the aptly named Flyte model. Roughly echoing the shape of Gibson's Flying V from the late 1950s, the Flyte's arrowhead outline and pointed headstock clearly suggest an object that wants to be airborne.

Electric guitar

(M-1 model)
GRD
United States (South Strafford, Vermont), about 1978–80

DURING THE 1970S, many people fed up with urban living tried retreating to rural settings in an effort to "get back to the land." When shoveling compost proved to be less than satisfying, some turned to more creative pursuits like woodworking and gravitated to central Vermont. There, an artist and talented guitar maker named Charles Fox (born 1943) had founded a residential guitar-building program in 1973 called the Guitar Research and Design Center. GRD was the first such school established in North America, and in 1978 some of its graduates began to manufacture instruments for sale to "creative musicians" (as their advertising put it). Besides GRD's acoustic models, Fox designed three styles of solid-body electric guitar. The inspiration for the concave headstock of the M-1 model was taken from Panormo guitars of the 1820s, but a so-called Omega cutout was added to the center. Enlarging and inverting this design became the basis for the body as well. Like the work of many '70s artisans, GRD guitars reveled in the beauty of wood, using boldly grained species like rosewood accented with brass fittings.

Minimalism

THE URGE TOWARD ORNAMENTATION often runs parallel with an impulse to simplify, to strip an object down to its essentials, and there has been no exception with the guitar, especially in the twentieth century. Usually it is the aesthetic elements that are simplified, eliminating extraneous decoration and streamlining the body. In many examples, the construction principles and technical components have been thoroughly rethought as well, and a frequent by-product of this reduction process is a lighter and more portable guitar. The minimalistic approach also presents the creative mind with an engaging challenge, as one reconsiders the guitar's function and brings to bear first principles of design. And then there are those who simply enjoy the shock value of making things look radically different, forcing us to re-examine our relationship with material artifacts. Only a few of the minimal designs for guitars have become long-lasting successes, but all are interesting and help define the boundaries of what a guitar can or cannot be.

ELECTRIC GUITAR

(2 × 4 model)

La Baye Company

United States (Green Bay, Wisconsin), 1967

THE BODY DIMENSIONS of the 2 × 4 model, named after the mainstay of construction lumber, are indeed very close to being two by four inches, although a nice chunk of mahogany was used rather than the fir and hemlock found in house frames. While living in Green Bay, Wisconsin, guitarist and teacher Dan Helland reasoned that an electric guitar was essentially a fingerboard, strings, and an electronic pickup. So why not just mount these components to a block of wood? Les Paul had done the same thing thirty years earlier, but he masked the 4 × 4 body of his "Log" (as he called it) with removable halves of a hollow-body guitar. Helland's 2 × 4 was completely functional, came in seven color schemes, and was available as a six-string, twelve-string, or bass instrument. The idea was in step with certain trends of the time, but the look was just too radical and the execution too ugly for buyers, despite some short-lived exposure by Tommy James and the Shondells. Just as most car owners are disinclined to drive something that looks too much like a box, guitar players generally prefer an instrument with at least a little flair. Holman-Woodel, Inc., of Neodesha, Kansas, assembled only forty-five 2 × 4 guitars for the La Baye Company in 1967, after which this homely experiment slipped quietly into oblivion.

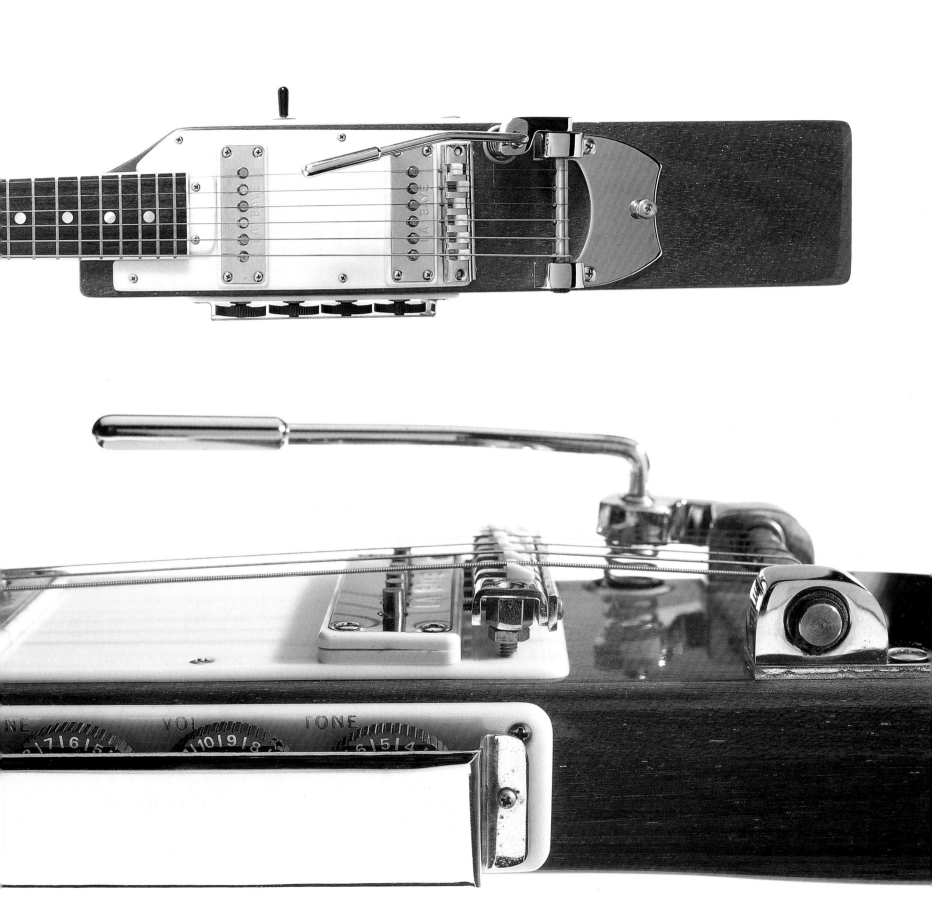

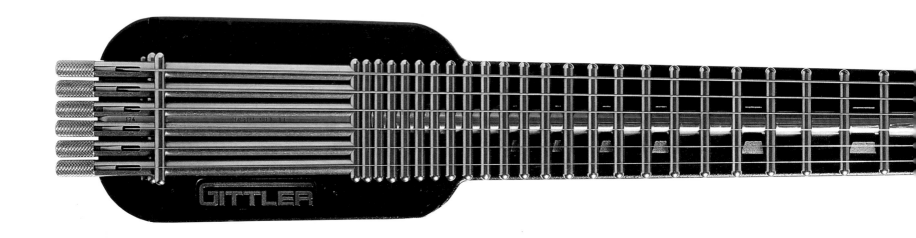

AMONG ATTEMPTS TO REINVENT the electric guitar in a dramatically new way, few have produced an instrument with such a startling appearance as one created by Alan Gittler. A guitarist/inventor/artist working in New York City in the early 1970s, Gittler initially designed a prototype with a skeletal metal framework, composed only of the shiny metal rods seen on this much later example. An elegant and sculptural form, a Gittler guitar was purchased by the Museum of Modern Art in 1977, making it the first musical instrument to enter their collection. It was Gittler's feeling that by paring the guitar down to its most basic components, it would become more responsive to the nuances of the musician; but most guitarists found it a considerable challenge to hold and play this curious invention. After moving to Israel in the early 1980s and changing his name to Avraham Bar Rashi, Gittler licensed Astron Engineering to continue manufacturing his instruments. However, in a manner that Gittler considers abhorrent to his original intentions, Astron began to add a small oval body to the minimalist metal framework, and then in later examples added a neck to help guide the player's left hand. Even in this fleshed-out model, though, the strings are pressed down between the frets and do not contact a fingerboard, a playing technique rather like that used on many string instruments from India. The Gittler guitar has always been considered an oddity, but one was played by Andy Summers of the Police in their video for "Synchronicity II."

ELECTRIC GUITAR
Astron Engineering Enterprises
Alan Gittler (born 1928)
Israel, about 1987

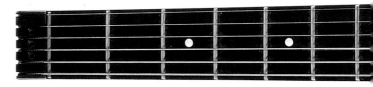

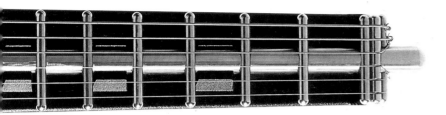

AWARD-WINNING industrial designer Ned Steinberger (born 1948) was not the first to radically rethink the form of the electric guitar, but he is considered to have been one of the most successful. Approaching the instrument without preconceptions, in 1981 he introduced his first important design for an electric bass, which, like this guitar, had a one-piece body and neck made from a "secret" formulation of epoxy resin, carbon graphite, and glass fibers. Twice as dense as wood and ten times stiffer, this reinforced plastic is stronger than steel and lacks the inconsistency that results in tonally dead spots in wood-bodied instruments. The instrument looks small, but the strings are actually the same length as more traditional electric guitars. The deception results from eliminating the headstock altogether and attaching the strings to small knurled tuners very near the end of the trapezoidal body. Design journals praised the sleek, high-tech look, and musicians concurred that the sound was clear and the physical balance admirable, even if the artistically pure form was a bit disorienting and the price rather steep. Steinberger instruments have found some notable advocates, including Reeves Gabrels, who owns this L-series guitar and played it on many of the album tracks recorded in the late '80s with David Bowie.

ELECTRIC GUITAR

(GL2T model)
Steinberger Sound Company
United States (Newburgh, New York), 1986

TRAVEL GUITAR
(customized Backpacker model)
Made by Robert McNally for the Martin Guitar Company
United States (Nazareth, Pennsylvania), 1994

RELATIVE PORTABILITY is one of the guitar's best features, but over the centuries luthiers have nonetheless tried many different schemes for creating an ever more compact instrument. Several portable guitars are currently available on the market, from acoustic models with nylon or steel strings to solid-body electrics. The most successful and recognizable portable instrument is Martin's Backpacker model, originally designed by Robert McNally (born 1948). Since its introduction early in 1994, this diminutive but practical instrument has traveled the far reaches of the globe, from the North and South Poles to expeditions up Mount Everest. On March 14, 1994, this particular Backpacker instrument boldly went where no guitar has gone before: on board NASA's Columbia Space Shuttle as part of the personal luggage of mission specialist Pierre J. Thuot. It was a great publicity idea, but McNally had to create a customized instrument about a foot shorter than the thirty-six-inch standard model in order to meet the shuttle's storage restrictions. As is typical of shuttle equipment, the guitar was fitted with Velcro strips on the back, allowing it to be anchored to surfaces in the zero-gravity atmosphere of space.

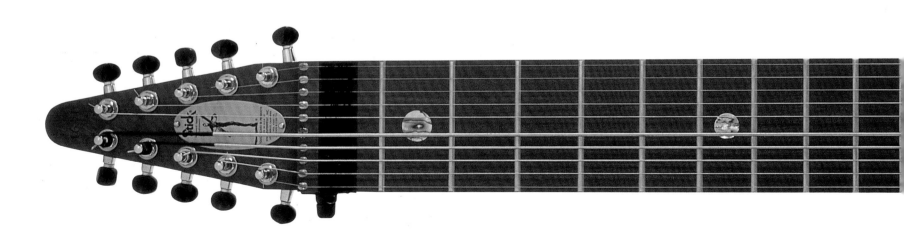

CHAPMAN STICK

Stick Enterprises, Inc.
United States (Woodland Hills, California), 2000

When I play well, I can be transported by the music. Everything else in the universe disappears. In addition to being a diversion, a tool to open doors socially, a course to conquer, a companion, and a source of pride, the guitar is my vehicle to a joy that is difficult to explain.

— DAVID BROMBERG

IN THE LATE 1960s, jazz guitarist Emmett Chapman (born 1936) took advantage of a guitar technique wherein the strings of an electrically amplified instrument need not be plucked, but can instead be played by percussively fretting a note against the fingerboard. By 1969 he had built his first "Stick" to further exploit this unique tapping technique. An instrument that is both worn and held to become "a part of your music making body," it allows a player to use both hands to play notes on the fingerboard. The result is a full and elaborate texture of melody, bass, and chords. The instrument has a very percussive tone quality with a long natural sustain. Stick Enterprises was founded in 1974 to manufacture and sell the Chapman Stick, which is available in eight-string, ten-string, and twelve-string models. Although the playing skills are considerably different from those employed on the traditional guitar, some notable performers have adopted the Stick, including Peter Gabriel and Tony Levin of the band King Crimson. A modified version of a Chapman Stick also appeared in the 1984 cult film *Dune*.

THE 1980s

BY THE 1980S, THE SOLID-BODY ELECTRIC GUITAR had come to dominate the popular music scene, as more musicians than ever used it to express an ever-increasing range of styles. So prevalent was electric music that even respected makers of acoustic instruments struggled to maintain a market for their products. The heavy-metal rock genre in particular reached new heights of popularity with groups like Guns 'N Roses and Def Leppard, often called "hair bands" because of their overtly hirsute appearance. The idea of the rock guitar hero still lingered in the '80s, and stars such as Eddie Van Halen and Steve Vai continued to stretch the boundaries of electric guitar playing with pyrotechnics that would have made Paganini proud.

But the days were numbered for rock bands built around the talents of a single guitarist, as groups such as the Police showed that economy of musical gesture could often produce more satisfying results. Rap music, although not structured around the guitar, paved the way for sound "sampling," which was quickly adopted as a new means of expression. Ultimately, many fans were beginning to value musicianship and a good tune more than pure technique.

The search for the perfect guitar continued throughout the 1980s, although much of it progressed along the traditional routes mapped out during previous decades. A versatile sound palette offered by synthesizer guitars looked promising at first, but regular electric instruments ultimately resisted the incursion. New materials like graphite were tried out for guitar bodies and necks, but their expense made development costly and often placed the final product out of reach for many buyers. Only a few breakthroughs in visual or mechanical design were in evidence, but the craft of manufacturing guitars steadily improved among makers of both electric and acoustic models, in America and abroad. As with many other products whose fundamental technology was essentially worked out, the only way to maintain interest from consumers was to restyle the product's visual appeal. But the beauty of even the best new guitar designs was typically lost on the average player, who still spent hard-earned dollars on one of the same tried-and-true models that had always been popular.

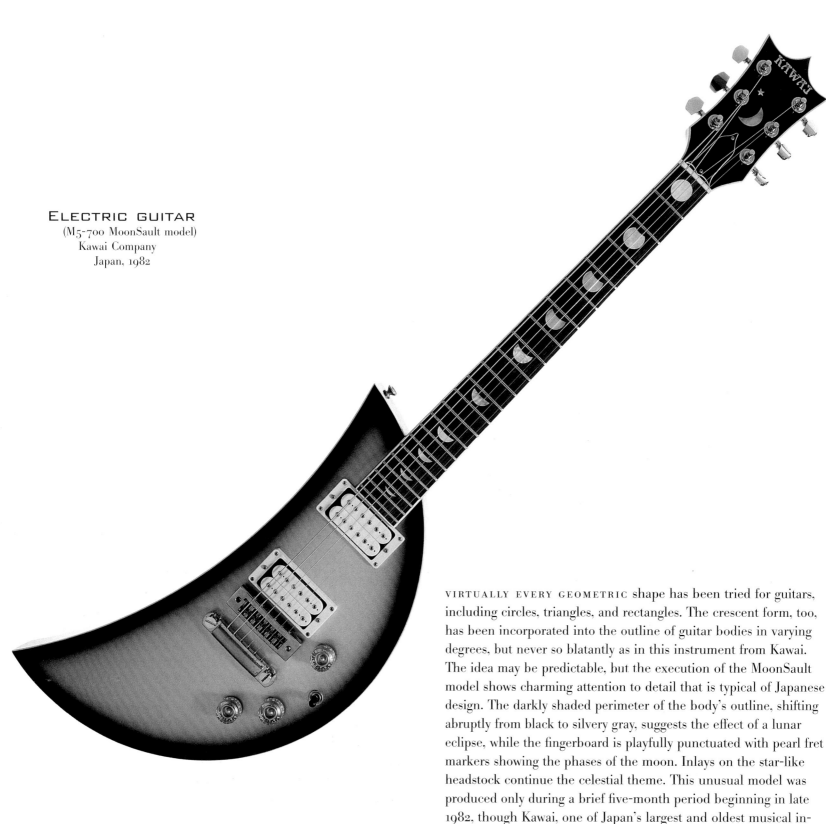

ELECTRIC GUITAR
(M5-700 MoonSault model)
Kawai Company
Japan, 1982

VIRTUALLY EVERY GEOMETRIC shape has been tried for guitars, including circles, triangles, and rectangles. The crescent form, too, has been incorporated into the outline of guitar bodies in varying degrees, but never so blatantly as in this instrument from Kawai. The idea may be predictable, but the execution of the MoonSault model shows charming attention to detail that is typical of Japanese design. The darkly shaded perimeter of the body's outline, shifting abruptly from black to silvery gray, suggests the effect of a lunar eclipse, while the fingerboard is playfully punctuated with pearl fret markers showing the phases of the moon. Inlays on the star-like headstock continue the celestial theme. This unusual model was produced only during a brief five-month period beginning in late 1982, though Kawai, one of Japan's largest and oldest musical instrument companies, first began making guitars in 1956.

ELECTRIC GUITAR
(Pro II U series Urchin Deluxe model)
Arai Company (Aria trademark)
Japan, 1984

THE MENACING PRONGS on the Urchin guitar might be inspired by the spiny points of the instrument's sea-dwelling namesake, or they might suggest the sinister fins of a shark. Either way, it is not hard to see an aquatic motif at work here, with a deeply shaded blue-black varnish over a stripe-figured maple veneer that suggests ripples in a sandy beach as the ocean breaks over it. Glowing gold-plated hardware heightens the instrument's sensuous appeal. Various other guitar models from the 1980s also tried out the pointy look (what some makers refer to as "eye-pokers"), as heavy-metal bands sometimes used their instrument's weapon-like appearance as a visual complement to the loud, thrashing music that was their trademark. Introduced in 1981, the Urchin was Arai's first weird-shaped model, probably inspired by the work of B. C. Rich, a California guitar maker who had started building guitars with dramatic curves and cutaways a decade earlier. Despite its adventurous styling, the Urchin never sold as well as the company's more traditionally shaped copies of classic American guitars.

ELECTRIC GUITAR

(Triaxe model)
Kramer (BKL) Company
United States (Neptune, New Jersey), 1986

THE POPULARITY OF outer-space adventure stories has ebbed and flowed since the first *Flash Gordon* films of the late 1930s. But the 1980s witnessed a particularly strong surge of interest in science fiction as the famous *Star Trek* television series of the '60s was revived on both the large and small screen. Kramer's Triaxe model pays overt homage to the alien spaceships that do battle in these futuristic adventures. Shapes suggesting aircraft and motion have been a recurrent theme among guitar makers since Gibson first introduced the Flying V model in the late '50s. The Triaxe is much more than suggestive, though, with broad wings and a menacing headstock for a cockpit. Only a handful of these whimsical guitars were made, as the shape is clearly more for fun than for serious playing. The Kramer Company was founded in 1975 and flourished during the 1980s largely due to an endorsement by rock guitarist Eddie Van Halen. It was also the sole marketer of a locking tremolo system designed by player Floyd Rose, in which the strings can be made to go almost completely slack using the whammy bar, but will accurately return to their original pitch when the bar is released. Heavy-metal guitarists call this dramatic glissando effect "dive bombing."

187

DIGITAL GUITAR

(DG1 model)
Stepp Ltd.
England (London), about 1987

BOLDLY PROCLAIMED as "the logical step in the evolution of the guitar," Stepp's digital instrument underwent four long years of development before experiencing two short years of production. It is said to be one of the first self-contained guitar synthesizers because its synth voice boards, power supply, and communications interface are contained in a so-called LSU (Life Support Unit), which also handily functions as a stand for the guitar. The strings themselves, all of the same gauge, do not actually sound and do not require tuning. They are there to allow the player the familiarity of touch found in a normal guitar and to interact with the "semi-conductive intelligent frets" to transmit information about finger placement. As a synthesizer, the instrument can produce an incredible array of sounds, emulating guitars, pianos, strings, and winds, but the square plastic body and the touch-pad control panel give it an appearance of high-tech medical equipment. The DG1 was an expensive instrument, and was ultimately not as exciting for players as Stepp hoped it would be. Guitarist Steve Howe, best known for his work with the progressive rock group Yes, purchased this instrument new in 1987, but never managed to work out its idiosyncrasies enough to usefully employ it onstage or in the recording studio.

Most players accept guitar synthesizers at face value, whereas I always process the sounds as you would a guitar. I run them through fuzz tones and delay units to alter the synth sound even more.

— ADRIAN BELEW

Customization

CUSTOMIZATION HAS BEEN PRACTICED since the days of the very earliest guitars, which were most often built to order for a specific client. But even after luthiers developed standard models, they were always willing to create guitars with elaborate decoration for wealthy amateurs and with special technical specifications for discriminating players. Today, many major guitar manufacturers have separate shops devoted solely to custom work. Recent decades have witnessed some particularly interesting productions, as players have gotten more involved in the process of designing guitars that express their musical and visual tastes. A few performers, meanwhile, have taken matters into their own hands, such as Eddie Van Halen, who used rather low-tech means such as spray paint and tape to create his own unique-looking instruments.

ELECTRIC GUITAR

(Strawberry 6 custom model)
Mosrite Company
United States (Bakersfield, California), 1967

THIS UNIQUE GUITAR is one of the earliest examples of an instrument specifically designed to reinforce the image of a particular rock group, in this case the 1960s psychedelic band Strawberry Alarm Clock, a one-hit wonder with the tune "Incense and Peppermints." The group received this guitar in 1967 at the height of their short career, along with a matching red twelve-string and a purple bass. Built by guitar maker Semie Moseley (1935–1992), these were not just gimmicky props; the band used all three instruments extensively in both live and recorded performances. Moseley was a gifted designer of guitars, even though his numerous business ventures (including the Mosrite Company that produced this instrument) were less than long lasting. Vivid colors like the bright green on this fantastically shaped guitar were a hallmark of the psychedelic era, as were curvilinear forms inspired by the French Art Nouveau period. The swirling pinstriped detailing is similar to treatment found on custom hot rods of the time.

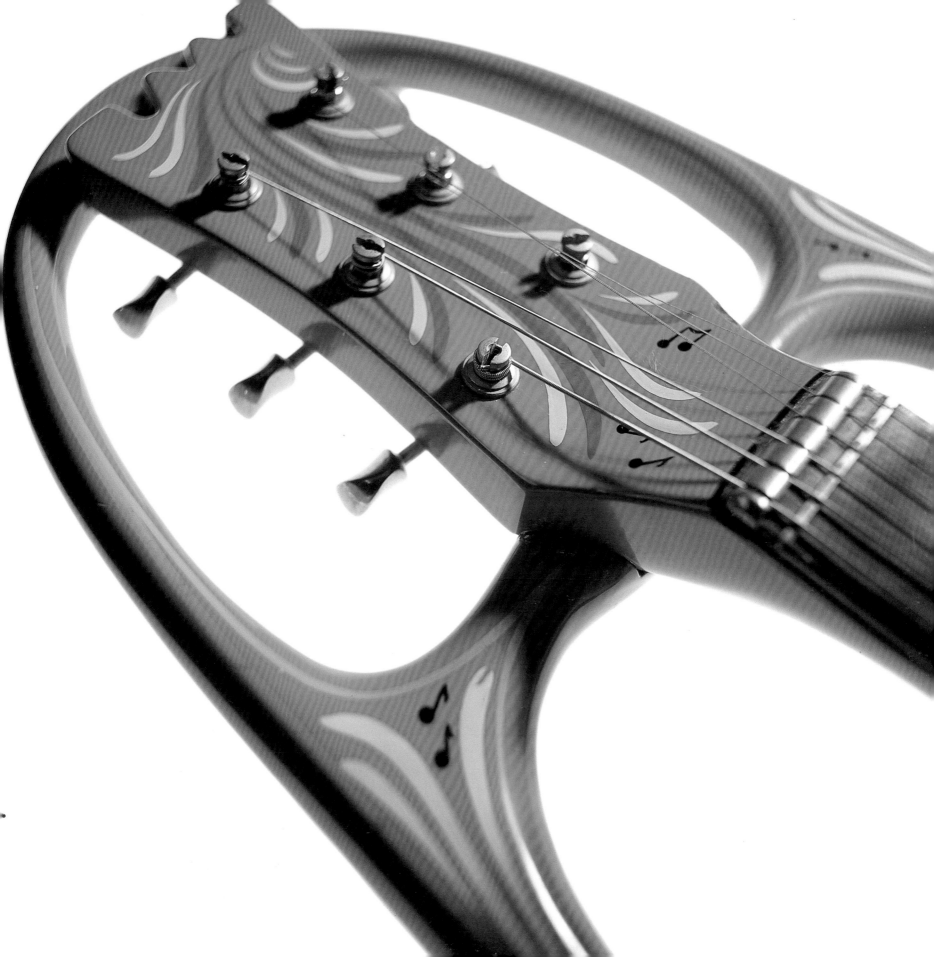

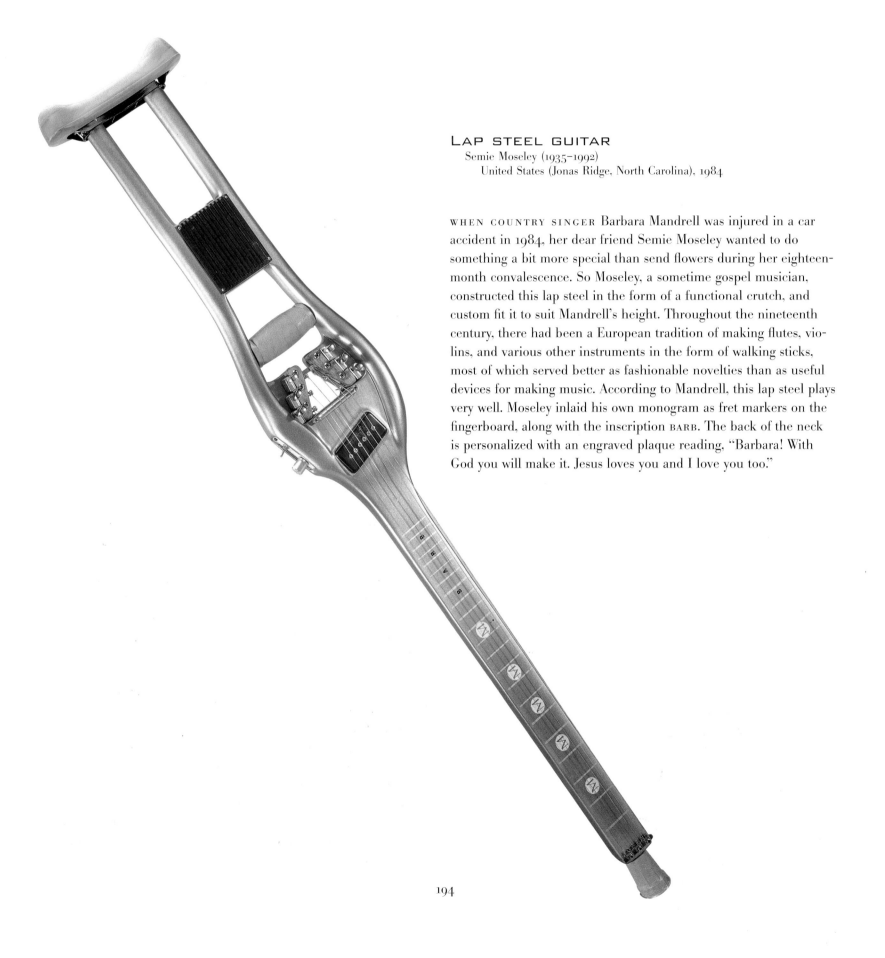

LAP STEEL GUITAR
Semie Moseley (1935–1992)
United States (Jonas Ridge, North Carolina), 1984

WHEN COUNTRY SINGER Barbara Mandrell was injured in a car accident in 1984, her dear friend Semie Moseley wanted to do something a bit more special than send flowers during her eighteen-month convalescence. So Moseley, a sometime gospel musician, constructed this lap steel in the form of a functional crutch, and custom fit it to suit Mandrell's height. Throughout the nineteenth century, there had been a European tradition of making flutes, violins, and various other instruments in the form of walking sticks, most of which served better as fashionable novelties than as useful devices for making music. According to Mandrell, this lap steel plays very well. Moseley inlaid his own monogram as fret markers on the fingerboard, along with the inscription BARB. The back of the neck is personalized with an engraved plaque reading, "Barbara! With God you will make it. Jesus loves you and I love you too."

ELECTRIC GUITAR

(Yellow Cloud model)
David Rusan and Barry Haugen
of Knut-Koupee Enterprises, Inc.
United States (Minneapolis, Minnesota), 1989

THE POP MUSICIAN originally called Prince (Prince Rogers Nelson) has always cultivated a flamboyant persona in his music, costume, lifestyle, and even choice of name. This multitalented funk-rock star changed his name in 1993 to an unpronounceable glyph that overlays the symbols for man and woman into a single icon, causing the press to now refer to him as "the artist formerly known as Prince." One of his stage instruments is an attention-grabbing guitar built in the actual shape of this symbol, but he also plays examples of his so-called Cloud model, a design he has had manufactured in varying colors by guitar makers in his hometown of Minneapolis. Immediately recognizable by a long, undulating extension from the upper edge of the body, the guitar features sensual contours that serve to accentuate the androgynous performer's penchant for overt sexuality in both his music and his stage antics. The fret markers inlaid in the fingerboard are a basic version of what eventually became the artist's name/symbol. Formerly owned by the impish rocker himself, this guitar was donated to the Smithsonian Institution in 1993 to be preserved with countless other pop culture artifacts, from Dorothy's ruby slippers to Muhammad Ali's boxing gloves.

195

ELECTRIC GUITAR

(five-neck custom model)
Hamer Guitars, Inc.
United States (Arlington Heights, Illinois), 1981

THIS EXERCISE IN EXCESS is owned by guitarist Rick Nielsen of the pop-rock band Cheap Trick, and was played by him during many years of touring with the group. It was stolen in Australia in 1988, but resurfaced two months later in Detroit (and eventually was replaced by another Hamer five-neck covered with the band's trademark pattern of black and white checkerboard). Nielsen has long been an avid collector of vintage electric guitars, and has also commissioned several unusual custom instruments like this one from Hamer Guitars, whose factory was once located near his hometown of Rockford, Illinois. Working with Jol Dantzig, one of Hamer's founders, Nielsen thought to caricature other rock guitarists of the '70s, whose hackneyed idea of cool was double-necked instruments. He envisioned a guitar that had six necks and would spin around as a theatrical effect, but five ended up being Dantzig's practical limit. Thirty-six strings are a lot to keep in tune, and the instrument is monstrously heavy, but the intent here was clearly more shock value than practicality. Nielsen's own take on his five-necked behemoth: "This guitar still gets more applause than I probably ever will."

196

ELECTRIC GUITAR

(Les Paul custom model)
Gibson Guitar Corp. (Custom Division)
United States (Nashville, Tennessee), 1995

KIX BROOKS, of the Nashville-based duo Brooks and Dunn, is originally from Louisiana, where he came to appreciate the primal beauty of alligators. To celebrate this passion on a guitar, Brooks went to Gibson's custom shop division, where he worked with carver Bruce J. Kunkel and others to design this unique instrument. Made from an extra-thick blank of mahogany, the body's high-relief carving was enhanced by an application of acrylic paint, while the half-submerged alligator inlaid into the fingerboard is composed of hundreds of carefully cut pieces of pearl and abalone shell. An especially humorous touch is supplied by control knobs carved as frogs, one of which is about to become lunch for a gator slithering around the rim of the body.

You don't want to play like B. B. King. You want to be you. So what you do is listen to players you like, and try to "borrow" a little bit from each guy. You don't try to sound exactly like the other guy, you just add the bits to your vocabulary. It's like learning to read or write.

— B. B. KING

GUITAR
(Pikasso model)
Linda Manzer (born 1952)
Canada (Toronto, Ontario), 1993

WHEN JAZZ ARTIST Pat Metheny asked Canadian instrument maker Linda Manzer to create a guitar with as many strings as possible, the result was dubbed the Pikasso. A guitar collector was so fascinated by the instrument that he had Manzer replicate it in a strictly acoustic version, without the electronic pickups incorporated into Metheny's instrument. With two soundholes, three necks, and forty-two strings in four groups, the Pikasso II is a tour-de-force of the luthier's art. The process of building the original instrument consumed five months of drawing time and another four of building. At almost twice the weight of a normal guitar, both Pikasso models are supplied with stands that support them for playing and display. Also unique is the wedge-shaped body, with sides thinner along the upper edge than the lower, allowing the player better access to the multiplicity of strings. Besides the regular six strings on its traditional neck, the three additional sets of twelve each are tuned to various schemes reflecting the note patterns of instruments such as the autoharp and Japanese koto, presenting the player with a considerable array of sound options.

Coat-hanger electric guitar

Ken Butler (born 1948)
United States (Brooklyn, New York), 1991

USING EVERY SORT OF "found object," from hockey sticks to umbrellas, artist Ken Butler combines his mixed materials in amusing and sometimes thought-provoking ways. Called by one reviewer "the Dr. Seuss of new music," Butler discovered the sculptural possibilities of guitars and violins in the late 1970s. His first instrument was "a small hatchet that he converted into a playable violin by adding a fingerboard, tailpiece, strings, and a contact microphone. He has since made some 150 hybrid string instrument/sculptures. These objects might look like toys, but in fact they have a more serious musical and sociological purpose. Exploring the theme of hyper-utility in the objects and images that surround us, Butler coaxes sounds from his Dada-like contraptions that are far better than they might appear capable of producing. The guitar in particular appeals to him as "a potent androgynous image of the female form, male phallus, and hand-held weapon."

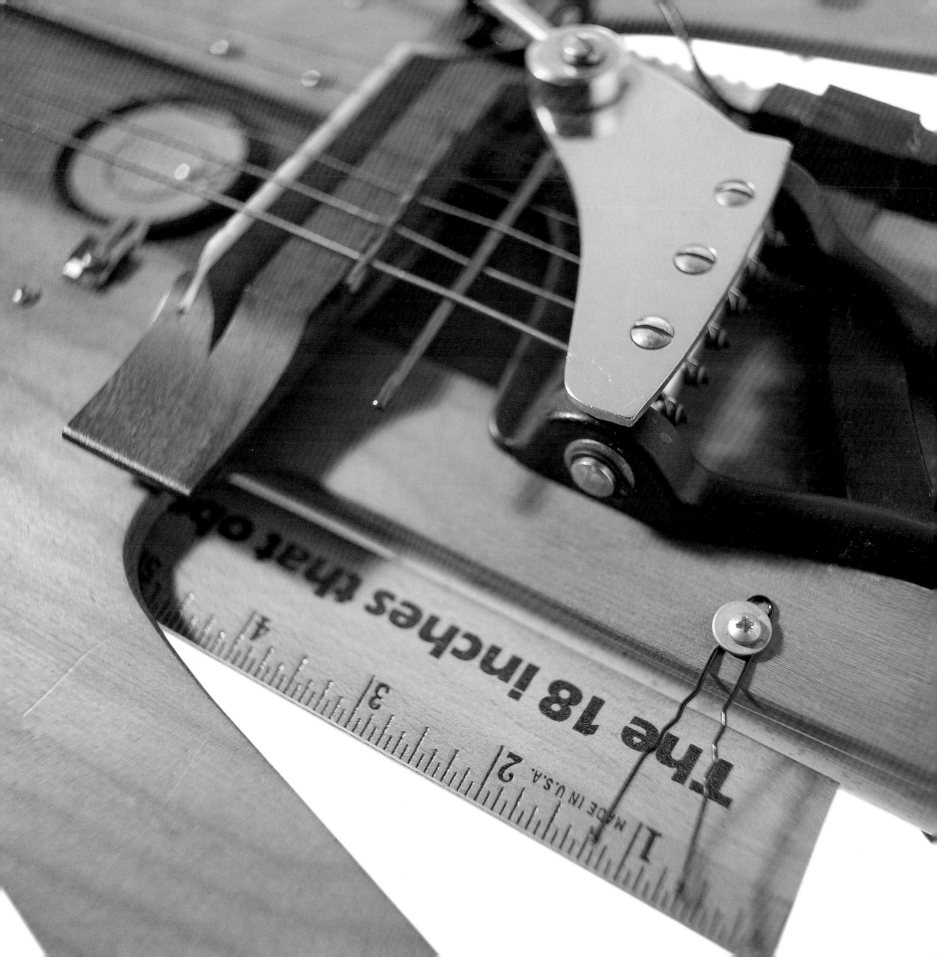

THE 1990s

AS THE TWENTIETH CENTURY CAME TO A CLOSE, nostalgia for music from earlier decades resulted in all manner of revivals. There were bands that overtly imitated the sound of their '60s rock and roll idols, and even '70s disco made a tongue-in-cheek comeback. Some groups, like the Grateful Dead, had never really stopped performing in thirty years, while others, like Yes and Santana, made successful comebacks. Blues, jazz, and swing enjoyed a resurgence of interest. Above all, though, the 1990s were a time of tremendous musical diversity. As the world became an increasingly smaller place, musical styles cross-fertilized, with American pop freely borrowing ethnic rhythms and harmonies from around the globe, and other cultures adopting instruments such as the electric guitar to newly interpret their own musical language.

Closer to home, so-called grunge bands such as Nirvana and Green Day resurrected the sound of basic rock and roll, while acknowledged masters of the electric instrument, such as Eric Clapton, showed off their considerable acoustic talents in a series of "unplugged" performances. And several female guitarists established their own dominion in this typically male preserve, including blues performer Bonnie Raitt and folk/pop artist Ani DiFranco.

During the 1990s, the craft of guitar making reached new levels of excellence, which continue unabated as we begin the present century. Never before has there been such a large number of high-quality new guitars from which to choose, whether classical, steel-string, electric, or even resonators. The rebirth of making arch-top guitars was perhaps the biggest success story, as this select field now boasts a greater number of talented builders than ever before. A demand for early electric guitars during the '90s created a phenomenal market for vintage instruments, and likewise led to a burgeoning industry in reissues of particularly popular models. But companies like PRS and Parker have proven that the guitar industry has yet to exhaust its ability to create new and successful types of instruments. No one can predict what kind of music the world will be listening to during the next hundred years, but it seems likely that, in one form or another, the guitar will continue to be part of our musical heritage for a long time to come.

ELECTRIC GUITAR

(Dragon 2000 model)
PRS Guitars
United States (Stevensville, Maryland), 1999

THE SOLID-BODY GUITARS designed by Paul Reed Smith (born
1956) are a fusion of the double-horned form of Fender's classic
Stratocaster with the rounded shape and carved, figured-maple top
of Gibson's equally famous Les Paul model. However, it is primarily
precise craftsmanship and careful wood selection that has made PRS
instruments among the most highly regarded production electrics of
present times. Smith built his first guitar in 1975 for a college music
class, and a short ten years later was shipping his "vintage style"
guitars from a new factory in Maryland. His aim is to recapture the
sound of great electric guitars from the '50s and '60s, using specially
made pickups and old-fashioned hide glue rather than modern syn-
thetics. A teenage dream of Smith's was to build a guitar featuring a
dragon in its decoration, a fantasy that was first realized in 1992 with
the creation of the Dragon I series, a limited-edition instrument
with the creature intricately inlaid into the fingerboard. Increasingly
elaborate Dragon models were issued in the following two years,
and the Dragon 2000 represents the most ornate and possibly last
manifestation of Smith's vision, with an incredibly lavish version of
the mythical beast covering the body itself. Among the many professional guitarists who have adopted PRS instruments, the most visible
endorser is Carlos Santana.

ELECTRIC GUITAR

(Fly Artist model)
Parker Guitars
United States (Wilmington, Massachusetts), 1999

DURING FIFTEEN YEARS in the guitar repair field, Ken Parker (born 1952) studied the construction and problems of every instrument on the market. Armed with that knowledge, he began designing his own model of electric guitar in 1991, playfully dubbed the Fly by Larry Fishman, Parker's collaborator and a leading designer of pickups for acoustic guitars. Drawing inspiration from boats, cars, planes, and sports equipment, Parker employed his talents as a woodcarver to create the Fly's novel shape, which some describe as futuristic. But the sculptural contours of the body also produce an ergonomic instrument that is well balanced and comfortable for the player; at five pounds, the Fly is about half the weight of Gibson's popular Les Paul model. Parker guitars contain numerous technical innovations, but are best known for the patented use of extremely thin layers of high-modulus carbon and glass fiber applied to the back of the body and neck to create a unified, lightweight exoskeleton. Despite the use of such space-age materials, the bodies of all Parker guitars are made from solid planks of high-quality tone woods, including poplar, mahogany, ash, or spruce, each chosen for its properties of musical response and sustained tone. The various Fly models are rapidly catching on with well-known players such as Joe Walsh and Paul Simon.

ACOUSTIC/ELECTRIC GUITAR

(Chet Atkins SC model)
    Gibson Guitars
        United States (Nashville, Tennessee), 1993

AFTER ENDORSING GRETSCH guitars for over twenty-five years, versatile guitarist Chet Atkins changed allegiance and signed on with Gibson in 1981. The first project with his new partner was to develop an idea he had long been considering, which was to create a classical-type guitar with nylon strings that could be electrically amplified. Atkins had been experiencing trouble with weak finger-nails that chipped and broke when playing steel-string instruments, so he preferred the gentler feel of nylon strings, but still needed amplification to record and play in public venues. Gibson introduced various versions of the idea starting in 1982, all of which are classi-fied as thin-line electro-acoustic guitars. The first Chet Atkins CE models (Classical Electric) were essentially solid, with a strictly cos-metic soundhole and a fingerboard that had the same two-inch width as a traditional classical instrument. Owned by Atkins himself, this later SC version (Studio Classic) is hollow and has no soundhole, but retains the open, slotted headstock of a classical guitar. Piezo electronic pickups located in the bridge allow the instrument to be amplified with standard equipment, though it also produces consid-erable sound unplugged. Guitars with a similar body construction but steel strings were added to Gibson's line starting in 1987, and have found favor with players such as Dave Matthews.

PROTOTYPE GUITAR

(Opus 103)
William "Grit" Laskin (born 1953)
Canada (Toronto, Ontario), 1989

WILLIAM LASKIN, better known to friends as "Grit," is one of North America's premier independent makers of flat-top guitars. He is best known for his extraordinarily detailed use of multicolored, engraved inlay on his fingerboards and headstocks, each custom made and often depicting a scene or motifs that are significant to the instrument's owner. In 1989 Laskin created this startling prototype for a guitar in which the strings intersect the top at a quite steep angle, as they do with the soundboard of a harp. Similar experiments with string angle have been attempted since the nineteenth century, and there are other contemporary guitar builders who employ the same principle, although far less dramatically. Increasing the string angle makes the top much more of a strain-bearing structure and substantially changes the sound. The shape of Laskin's guitar is physically awkward for the player, but hands-on experience by one performer reveals that the tone is quite full and "orchestral." Laskin has continued to consider how this design might be improved, but no further models have been constructed to date. Although some may find the acute bends of the Dali-esque body visually disturbing, it is a thought-provoking exploration of how the guitar's traditional configuration can be transformed.

ACOUSTIC/ELECTRIC GUITAR

(Chrysalis model)
Chrysalis Guitar Co., Inc.
United States (New Boston, New Hampshire), 1999

THE UNUSUAL LOOK of the Chrysalis guitar reflects an exciting intersection of interests for inventor Tim White (born 1950), who studied insect acoustics in college but has also long been fascinated by the science of guitar sound. He discovered long ago that the wing of a flying insect is one of the most efficient structures for moving air, which is essentially what the thin wood top of a guitar does to amplify the vibrations of its strings. After twenty years of wrestling with the idea, White began building instruments in which a naturalistic grid of graphite is substituted for a traditional plate of spruce. But to properly amplify the sound, there must also be a hollow, resonant chamber, supplied here by an inflatable Mylar balloon inside a fabric shell that attaches with Velcro to the guitar's graphite rim. Although the appearance of White's inflatable guitar always elicits a variety of comments, his main aim in designing it was to create a full-size acoustic/electric instrument that is extremely portable. When an aluminum cam lever on the back of the headstock is moved, the strings' tension is released and the neck can be removed from the body, which itself comes apart in halves. With the balloon deflated, the whole affair can be packed into a normal-sized attaché case.

But the guitar, my lady, whether well played or badly played, well strung or badly strung, is pleasant to hear and listen to; being so easy to learn, it attracts the busiest of talented people and makes them put aside loftier occupations so that they may hold a guitar in their hands.

— LUIS DE BRIÇEÑO

ARCH-TOP GUITAR

(Centura model)
James D'Aquisto (1935–1995)
United States (Greenport, New York), 1995

HIS CAREER CUT SHORT at the age of 60, Jimmy D'Aquisto is acknowledged as the creator of some of the finest and most original guitars of the twentieth century, and some say of all times. Having trained in the Manhattan workshop of renowned arch-top guitar maker John D'Angelico, he almost single-handedly kept the craft of arch-top guitar making alive for nearly a decade after his master's death in 1964. The earliest guitars made by D'Aquisto were modeled after those of his teacher, but by the 1970s he began to introduce modifications that would ultimately result in instruments that were distinctly his own. D'Aquisto gradually supplanted the flashy decoration and geometric hardware derived from the Art Deco style with simpler lines and gently curved forms that gave the guitar a much cleaner look overall. This included the use of wood tailpieces and pickguards, and the reduction or even elimination of edge binding and fingerboard inlays. This exquisite Centura model is the last guitar entered into D'Aquisto's shop ledger, and was all but complete when he died. The bridge, nut, and truss-rod cover were completed by John Monteleone, one of many arch-top guitar makers inspired by D'Aquisto's work, who strive to carry forward the high standards he set for his craft.

Glossary

ACOUSTIC GUITAR: A guitar in which the string vibrations are amplified by a thin, flexible top and resonate inside a hollow body.

ARCH-TOP GUITAR: An acoustic guitar in which the top and usually the back are shaped into a slight arch, either by carving or bending the wood. Arch-top guitars invariably have steel strings that are attached to a tailpiece.

BINDING: Wood, plastic, or other material along the edges of a guitar's top, back, and fingerboard that is both decorative and protective. Sometimes called purfling, especially for inner layers of binding.

BOUTS: The convex and concave curves of a traditional guitar body. The concave portion, sometimes called the middle bout, is also referred to as the waist.

BRACES: Thin wood strips glued to the inside surfaces of an acoustic guitar's top and back to give them support. Top bracing occurs in several patterns, including lateral, fanned, and crisscross. Also called struts.

BRIDGE: A wood, metal, or composite structure attached to a guitar's top, which positions the strings at the proper height above the fingerboard and determines one end of their sounding length. On an acoustic guitar the bridge transmits the string vibrations to the top to amplify their sound. In some guitars the strings are attached directly to the bridge, while in others they pass over the bridge and are attached to a tailpiece or the end of the body.

CLASSICAL GUITAR: An acoustic guitar, traditionally of waisted shape, in which the treble strings are gut or nylon. To modern players, the term more specifically denotes a guitar made in the general style and proportions of instruments developed in Spain during the mid-nineteenth century.

ELECTRIC GUITAR: An instrument in which the string vibrations are amplified principally by electric pickups rather than by a thin, flexible top.

FINGERBOARD: A slab of wood or other hard material affixed to the neck's upper surface, against which the strings are pressed between the frets to change their pitch. Also called fretboard.

FLAMENCO GUITAR: An acoustic guitar of the same general size and shape as a classical guitar, but traditionally made from cypress wood and often using wood tuning pegs rather than geared tuning machines.

FLAT-TOP GUITAR: In modern usage the term "flat-top" denotes an acoustic guitar in which the top is flat and the strings are metal. The term is used in particular to differentiate this type from classical and arch-top guitars.

FRET MARKERS: Dots or other decorative devices inlaid into the fingerboard between certain frets to help orient the player to their hand position along the neck. Also called position markers.

FRETS: Raised strips placed across the fingerboard, between which the strings are pressed to produce different notes. In early guitars the frets were lengths of gut tied around the neck, but beginning in the late 1700s, frets were made of metal, ivory, or other hard material attached to the fingerboard. Frets on Hawaiian guitars serve only as visual markers, since the strings are not pressed down to the fingerboard.

GOLPEADOR: On a flamenco guitar, a thin wood or plastic plate glued to the top to protect it from rhythmic finger tapping, which is a traditional element of flamenco-style playing.

HAWAIIAN GUITAR: A guitar in which the strings are positioned high above the fingerboard, and a metal bar held in the left hand is pressed against them to select different notes while the right hand plucks them with picks. Hawaiian guitars are placed flat across the lap. Also called steel guitar.

HEADSTOCK: An extension beyond the neck that carries tuning pegs or tuning machines to which the strings are attached. Also called peghead.

HEEL: The foot-shaped portion of the neck where it attaches to the body.

LAP STEEL GUITAR: In modern usage, a Hawaiian guitar that is electrically amplified.

LUTHIER: An old French term originally denoting a lute maker, which later came to mean one who constructs string instruments in general. The term is now sometimes used even more broadly to define builders of any kind of musical instrument, but guitar manufacturers have adopted it more often than others.

NECK: A slender, handle-like piece of wood or other rigid material projecting from the body's upper end, over which the strings lie.

NUT: A ridge of wood, ivory, or other hard material inserted at the junction of the neck and headstock, which positions the strings at the proper height above the fingerboard and determines one end of their sounding length. Notches in the nut provide lateral string spacing.

PICKGUARD: A plate of plastic, wood, or other hard material attached to the body along the treble side of the strings to protect the top from wear by a pick. Also called scratch plate.

PICKUP: An electronic device that amplifies the string vibrations of a guitar. Pickups include the electromagnetic type, in which vibrations of steel strings affect a magnetic field to induce an alternating current, and the piezo-electric transducer, which converts movements of the top or bridge into electrical impulses.

RESONATOR GUITAR: A guitar with a metal or wood body in which the string vibrations are transmitted to one or more shallow dishes of spun aluminum to amplify their sound.

ROSE (ROSETTE): A decorative pattern of marquetry around the perimeter of a circular soundhole, especially on classical and flamenco guitars. The term "rose" or "rosette" is also used to denote a pierced wood or parchment disc covering the soundhole, or a tiered and sunken structure of pierced parchment attached inside the soundhole.

SOLID-BODY GUITAR: A guitar in which the body is made from essentially solid pieces of wood or other hard material and the string vibrations are amplified electronically.

SOUNDHOLE: Any opening in a guitar's top, back, or sides that allows sound to exit from the body, enhancing both tone and volume.

SOUNDING LENGTH: The portion of a string that vibrates, between the bridge and the nut.

STEEL GUITAR: See Hawaiian guitar.

TAILPIECE: A metal or wood fixture affixed to a guitar's lower end, to which the strings are attached after passing over the bridge.

TOP: The uppermost surface of a guitar's body, upon which the strings and bridge lie. Also called the soundboard, belly, or table.

TREMOLO: A mechanical device on certain electric guitars for slackening the strings to create a sudden lowering of pitch, varying from a slight waver to a deep glissando. Sometimes called a whammy bar, which also refers specifically to the lever used to activate the tremolo.

TUNING KNOBS: That part of a tuning peg or tuning machine gripped by the player when tuning the strings. Also called tuning buttons.

TUNING MACHINES: Devices for tuning the strings in which turning a knob transfers motion via metal gears to a cylindrical roller around which a string is wrapped.

TUNING PEGS: Pegs made of wood, ivory, or other hard material that fit snugly into holes in the headstock. Strings are wrapped around the shank of the pegs and can be adjusted for tension by turning the pegs.

WAIST: See bouts.

WHAMMY BAR: See tremolo.

CHECKLIST

PAGE 25 Guitar
Attributed to Belchior Dias
Portugal (Lisbon), about 1590
Rosewood, spruce, ebony, ivory
37¾ × 10 × 3⅝ in. (95.7 × 25.4 × 9.2 cm)
Collection of Frank and Leanne Koonce

PAGE 26 Guitar
Jacopo Checchucci
Italy (Livorno), 1628
Ebony, spruce, ivory
35⅜ × 10 × 4¾ in. (90 × 25.5 × 12 cm)
Tony Bingham

PAGE 28 Guitar
Attributed to Jakob Ertel
Italy (Rome), about 1690
Ebony, spruce, fruitwood, ivory, bone
35¾ × 9⅜ × 3⅞ in. (90.7 × 23.6 × 9.8 cm)
The Metropolitan Museum of Art;
Purchase, Rogers Fund, Mrs. Peter
Nicholas, University of Chicago Club of
New York, Mrs. Henry J. Heinz II and
Lowell S. Smith and Sally Sanford Gifts,
The Crosby Brown Collection of Musical
Instruments, by exchange, and funds
from various donors 1984

PAGE 31 Guitar
Nicholas Alexandre Voboam II
(after 1633–about 1693)
France (Paris), 1680
Ebony, cypress, spruce, ivory
36¼ × 9⅞ × 3¾ in. (91.9 × 25 × 9.3 cm)
Museum of Fine Arts, Boston;
Otis Norcross Fund, Gift of Mr. and
Mrs. Richard M. Fraser, and Bequest of
Gertrude T. Taft, by exchange 1993.576

PAGE 31 Guitar
Nicholas Alexandre Voboam II
(after 1633–about 1693)
France (Paris), 1693
Tortoiseshell, spruce, ebony, ivory
34⅜ × 10⅜ × 5⅞ in.
(87.5 × 26.5 × 15.1 cm)
Musée de la Musique–Cité de la Musique

PAGE 32 Guitar
Antonio Stradivari (1644–1737)
Italy (Cremona), 1700
Maple, spruce, ebony, ivory
36⅛ × 10½ × 3½ in.
(91.7 × 26.7 × 8.9 cm)
America's Shrine to Music Museum, The
University of South Dakota, Vermillion
(No. 2976, Rawlins Fund, 1985)

PAGE 33 Guitar
Antoine Aubry (active 1778–1784)
France (Mirecourt), 1779
Maple, spruce, ebony, applewood, ivory,
tortoiseshell, mother-of-pearl
35½ × 10⅜ × 4⅛ in.
(90.2 × 26.1 × 10.4 cm)
America's Shrine to Music Museum, The
University of South Dakota, Vermillion
(No. 5581, Rawlins Fund, 1993)

PAGE 37 Guitar
Attributed to Gennaro Fabricatore I
(active 1773–1832)
Italy (Naples), about 1805
Maple, spruce, ebony, ivory, mother-
of-pearl
36⅝ × 10⅞ × 3⅜ in. (93 × 27.4 × 8.4 cm)
Edinburgh University Collection of
Historic Musical Instruments

PAGE 38 Guitar
José Pagés (born 1762)
Spain (Cadiz), 1813
Rosewood, spruce, ebony, mother-of-pearl,
ivory
39¾ × 11⅜ × 4⅜ in. (101 × 28.9 × 11.2 cm)
Edinburgh University Collection of
Historic Musical Instruments

PAGE 41 Guitar
Louis Panormo (1784–1862)
England (London), 1823
Maple, spruce, cedar, pearwood
37 × 11¼ × 3⅜ in. (94 × 28.5 × 8.6 cm)
Collection of Frank and Leanne Koonce

PAGE 43 Nine-string guitar
René François Lacôte (1785–1855)
France (Paris), 1827
Mahogany, spruce, ebony, whalebone
36¼ × 11⅞ × 3¾ in. (92 × 30 × 9.5 cm)
Museum of Fine Arts, Boston; Museum
purchase with funds donated anonymously
through the Joseph Bishop Van Sciver
Fund (1861–1943) of The Boston Foun-
dation and an anonymous donor 2000.629

PAGE 45 Guitar
Johann Georg Stauffer (1778–1853)
Austria (Vienna), about 1830
Maple, spruce
37⅞ × 11¼ × 3⅛ in. (96 × 28.5 × 8 cm)
Dennis Cinelli

PAGE 46 Guitar
Christian Frederick Martin (1796–1873)
United States (New York, New York),
1833–1840
Rosewood, spruce, ivory, mother-of-pearl,
abalone
37 × 11½ × 3⅜ in. (94 × 29.2 × 8.3 cm)
Courtesy of the Chinery Collection

PAGE 48 Guitar
Probably by Antoine Anciaume
(born 1776)
France (Mirecourt), about 1840
Amboyna wood, spruce, mother-of-pearl,
abalone
36 × 11¾ × 3¼ in. (91.5 × 29.6 × 8.1 cm)
Museum of Fine Arts, Boston; Museum
Purchase with funds donated anonymously
through the Joseph Bishop Van Sciver
Fund (1861–1942) of the Boston
Foundation 1999.520

PAGE 49 *Bambina* guitar
Possibly by D. & A. Roudhloff
England (London), about 1870
Rosewood, spruce, cedar, ebony
21⅜ × 5⅞ × 1¾ in. (54.3 × 14.8 × 4.2 cm)
Museum of Fine Arts, Boston; Museum
purchase with funds donated anonymously
through the Joseph Bishop Van Sciver
Fund (1861–1943) of The Boston Founda-
tion and an anonymous donor 2000.630

PAGE 52 Lyre guitar
Probably by François Gratel (born 1793)
France (Mirecourt), about 1810
Maple, spruce, ebony, mother-of-pearl
31¼ × 12⅞ × 3⅜ in.
(79.2 × 32.7 × 8.4 cm)
The Steve Howe Collection

PAGE 53 Lyre guitar
Pons fils
France (Paris), about 1810
Mahogany, spruce, ebony
34⅜ × 14⅜ × 4⅛ in. (87 × 36.6 × 10.5 cm)
The Metropolitan Museum of Art;
Purchase, Clara Mertens Bequest, in
memory of André Mertens 1998

PAGE 54 Lyre guitar (Apollo lyre)
Clementi and Company
England (London), about 1810
Maple, spruce, ebony, ivory
34⅜ × 14⅜ × 4⅛ in. (87 × 36.3 × 10.5 cm)
Philip Wigglesworth Cushing and Henry
Cowell Coolidge Wigglesworth, from the
collection of their parents, Frank and
Anne Wigglesworth

PAGE 55 Guitar-harp
Mordaunt Levien
France (Paris), about 1825
Maple, spruce, ebony, ivory
33⅛ × 12⅞ × 5⅞ in. (84 × 32.8 × 15 cm)
Museum of Fine Arts, Boston; Museum
purchase with funds donated by
Bradford M. and Dorothea R. Endicott
and an anonymous donor 2000.632

PAGE 56 Harp-guitar
Joseph Laurent Mast (active 1802–1830)
France (Toulouse), 1827
Maple, spruce, ebony
45 × 13¾ × 5¾ in.
(114.3 × 34.9 × 14.6 cm)
Courtesy of the Chinery Collection

PAGE 57 Harp-guitar
Emilius Nicolai Scherr
(1794–1874)
United States (Philadelphia, Pennsylvania),
1830s
Rosewood, spruce
59⅞ × 13 × 3⅜ in. (152 × 33 × 8.7 cm)
Smith College

PAGE 58 Harpo-lyre
André Augustin Chévrier
(active 1820–1842)
France (Paris), about 1830
Walnut, spruce, ebony, ivory
40⅝ × 20⅞ × 4⅛ in.
(103 × 53.1 × 10.5 cm)
Metropolitan Museum of Art; Purchase,
Mr. and Mrs. Thomas A. Cassilly Gift 1992

PAGE 59 *Wappengitarre* (shield-shaped
guitar)
Probably by Victorin Drassegg (1782–1847)
Austria (Bregenz), about 1835
Walnut, spruce, ebony
38⅝ × 12¼ × 3 in. (98 × 31 × 7.5 cm)
Museum of Fine Arts, Boston; Museum
purchase with funds donated by Jeffrey
and Andrew Remis 2000.631

PAGE 62 Flamenco guitar
Antonio de Torres (1817–1892)
Spain (Seville), about 1858
Cypress, spruce, cedar, rosewood
38 × 12¾ × 3¾ in. (96.5 × 32.4 × 9.5 cm)
Courtesy of R. E. Bruné, luthier

PAGE 63 Flamenco guitar
Santos Hernández (1874–1943)
Spain (Madrid), 1934
Cypress, spruce, cedar, ebony
39½ × 14½ × 3¾ in.
(100.3 × 36.8 × 9.5 cm)
Courtesy of R. E. Bruné, luthier

PAGE 64 Classical guitar
Hermann Hauser I (1882–1952)
Germany (Munich), 1928
Rosewood, spruce, mahogany, ebony
38½ × 14¼ × 3¾ in.
(97.8 × 36.2 × 9.5 cm)
Courtesy of R. E. Bruné, luthier

PAGE 65 Classical guitar
Francisco Simplicio (1874–1932/3)
Spain (Barcelona), about 1929–30
Satinwood, spruce, cedar, ebony
39½ × 14¼ × 4 in.
(100.3 × 36.2 × 10.2 cm)
Courtesy of R. E. Bruné, luthier

PAGE 68 Flat-top guitar (Tilton model)
John C. Haynes and Company
United States (Boston, Massachusetts),
1880s
Rosewood, spruce, ebony, mother-of-pearl,
abalone, ivory
38 × 12 × 4¾ in. (96.5 × 30.6 × 12 cm)
Collection of James F. Bollman, Courtesy
of the Music Emporium

PAGE 69 Flat-top guitar
Probably by Lyon and Healy (Washburn
brand)
United States (Chicago, Illinois),
about 1900
Rosewood, spruce, ebony, mother-of-pearl,
abalone, ivory
37⅝ × 14 × 4⅜ in. (95.5 × 35.5 × 11.3 cm)
The Roy Acuff Collection, Gaylord
Entertainment, Nashville, Tennessee

PAGE 71 Arch-top guitar
Orville H. Gibson (1856–1918)
United States (Kalamazoo, Michigan),
about 1900
Walnut, spruce
40 × 15¾ × 2½ in. (101.6 × 40 × 6.4 cm)
Courtesy of the Chinery Collection

PAGE 72 Arch-top guitar (Style O Artist)
Gibson Mandolin-Guitar Company
United States (Kalamazoo, Michigan),
about 1918
Birch, spruce, ebony, plastic
38¼ × 16⅛ × 3⅜ in. (97.2 × 41 × 8.5 cm)
Fred Oster, Vintage Instruments,
Philadelphia

PAGE 74 Arch-top guitar with
sympathetic strings
Joseph Bohmann (1848–about 1930)
United States (Chicago, Illinois),
about 1910
Maple, spruce, ebony, ivory
37 × 12¾ × 3⅞ in. (94 × 32.2 × 9.8)
Stan Werbin, Elderly Instruments,
Lansing, Michigan

PAGE 78 Harp guitar
C. F. Martin and Company
United States (Nazareth, Pennsylvania),
about 1850–60
Rosewood, spruce, ebony
44 × 20 × 4⅜ in. (111.8 × 50.8 × 11.2 cm)
Gryphon Stringed Instruments, Palo Alto,
California

PAGE 81 Harp guitar (Style U)
Gibson Mandolin-Guitar Company
United States (Kalamazoo, Michigan), 1920
Birch, spruce, mahogany, ebony, plastic
45½ × 18¾ × 3½ in.
(115.6 × 47.6 × 8.9 cm)
Museum of Fine Arts, Boston; Museum
purchase with funds donated anonymously
2000.552

PAGE 83 Harp guitar (Symphony model,
style 8)
Made by Larson Brothers for distribution
by W. H. Dyer & Brother
United States (Chicago, Illinois),
about 1920
Mahogany, spruce, ebony, mother-of-
pearl, ivory
41½ × 15¾ × 4¼ in.
(105.4 × 40 × 10.8 cm)
Courtesy of the Chinery Collection

PAGE 84 Harp guitar
Harmony Company
United States (Chicago, Illinois),
about 1920s
Mahogany, spruce, ebony, mother-of-
pearl, plastic
50 × 15½ × 5⅛ in. (127 × 39.4 × 13 cm)
Alex Usher

PAGE 87 Guitar-lyre
Luigi Mozzani (1869–1943)
Italy (Cento), about 1910
Walnut, spruce, maple, ebony
38¾ × 18⅝ × 3¼ in.
(98.4 × 47.3 × 8.3 cm)
Courtesy of the Chinery Collection

PAGE 90 Flat-top guitar (D-45 model)
C. F. Martin and Company
United States (Nazareth, Pennsylvania),
1938
Rosewood, spruce, ebony, mother-of-pearl,
abalone, plastic
40¼ × 15¾ × 4⅞ in.
(102.2 × 40 × 12.5 cm)
Mac Yasuda

PAGE 91 Flat-top guitar (SJ-200 model)
Gibson, Inc.
United States (Kalamazoo, Michigan), 1938
Rosewood, spruce, ebony, mother-of-pearl,
plastic
42⅛ × 17 × 4⅞ in. (107 × 43.3 × 12.5 cm)
Mac Yasuda

PAGE 92 Flat-top guitar
Larson Brothers (Prairie State brand)
United States (Chicago, Illinois),
about 1935
Rosewood, spruce, mahogany, ebony,
mother-of-pearl, plastic
43 × 21 × 6⅛ in. (109.2 × 53.3 × 15.6 cm)
Courtesy of the Chinery Collection

PAGE 93 Bell-shaped guitar (5270 model)
Lyon and Healy (Washburn brand)
United States (Chicago, Illinois), about
1925–29
Mahogany, spruce, rosewood
36⅝ × 15⅝ × 3¾ in. (93 × 39.7 × 9.4 cm)
Stan Werbin, Elderly Instruments, Lansing,
Michigan

PAGE 94 Flat-top guitar (Rhumba model)
The Fred Gretsch Company, Inc.
United States (Brooklyn, New York),
about 1933–35
Mahogany, maple, spruce, ebony
36 × 16 × 3¼ in. (91.5 × 40.6 × 8.3 cm)
Courtesy of the Chinery Collection

PAGE 95 Cowboy guitar ("Singing
Cowboys" model)
Harmony Company
United States (Chicago, Illinois), 1942
Birch
36⅜ × 13¼ × 4¾ in.
(92.5 × 33.6 × 11.9 cm)
Brian Fischer

PAGE 98 Arch-top guitar
(L-5 Master Model)
Gibson, Inc.
United States (Kalamazoo, Michigan), 1924
Birch, maple, spruce, ebony, plastic
41 × 16 × 3½ in. (104.1 × 40.6 × 8.9 cm)
Courtesy of the Chinery Collection

PAGE 99 Electric arch-top guitar
(ES-150 model)
Gibson, Inc.
United States (Kalamazoo, Michigan), 1936
Maple, spruce, mahogany, rosewood,
plastic
40¾ × 16¼ × 3⅝ in.
(103.5 × 41.3 × 9.2 cm)
J. Geils

PAGE 100 Arch-top guitar (Orchestre
model)
Designed by Mario Maccaferri for
Selmer & Cie
France (Paris), 1932
Rosewood, spruce, ebony
38 × 15½ × 3⅞ in. (96.5 × 39.4 × 9.9 cm)
Courtesy of the Chinery Collection

PAGE 101 Arch-top guitar (Venetian
model, style A)
Kay Musical Instrument Company
(Kay-Kraft Brand)
United States (Chicago, Illinois),
about 1933
Mahogany, spruce, ebony, plastic
39¾ × 14⅜ × 3¾ in. (101 × 36.5 × 9.4 cm)
Michael Wright, The Different Strummer

PAGE 102 Arch-top guitar (Airway
W4 model)
Willi Wilkanowski (1886–about 1960)
United States (Brooklyn, New York), 1938
Maple, spruce, ebony, abalone, mother-
of-pearl
38 × 18 × 3¼ in. (96.5 × 45.7 × 8.3 cm)
Courtesy of Mars, The Musician's Planet

PAGE 103 Arch-top guitar (Super 400
model)
Gibson, Inc.
United States (Kalamazoo, Michigan), 1934
Maple, spruce, ebony, mother-of-pearl,
plastic
44 × 18 × 3½ in. (111.8 × 45.7 × 8.9 cm)
Courtesy of the Chinery Collection

PAGE 104 Arch-top guitar (Synchromatic
300 model)
The Fred Gretsch Company, Inc.
United States (Brooklyn, New York),
about 1946–49
Maple, spruce, ebony, mother-of-pearl,
plastic
43¼ × 17¼ × 3⅜ in.
(109.8 × 43.8 × 8.7 cm)
Scot Michael Arch

PAGE 105 Arch-top guitar (New Yorker
model)
John D'Angelico (1905–1964)
United States (New York, New York), 1954
Maple, spruce, ebony, mother-of-pearl,
plastic
43⅜ × 18 × 3¼ in. (110 × 45.6 × 8.2 cm)
Museum of Fine Arts, Boston; John H. and
Ernestine A. Payne Fund, and Harriet Otis
Cruft Fund 1998.62

PAGE 110 Hawaiian steel guitar (style 4)
Hermann C. Weissenborn (1863–1937)
United States (Los Angeles, California),
mid-1920s
Koa wood
37⅜ × 15⅜ × 2⅞ in. (94.8 × 39 × 7.3 cm)
Tim Scheerhorn

PAGE 111 Guitar (catalog model 49)
Stromberg-Voisinet Company
United States (Chicago, Illinois),
about 1932
Birch, spruce, basswood, plastic
36⅜ × 13¼ × 3¾ in.
(92.5 × 33.7 × 9.6 cm)
Michael Wright, The Different Strummer

PAGE 112 Stroh guitar (Hawaiian model)
Probably by George Evans and Company
England (London), about 1920
Mahogany, ebony, aluminum
39½ × 15 × 14 in. (100.3 × 38.1 × 35.6 cm)
Collection of Brian Cohen

PAGE 112 Resonator guitar (Tri-cone
model)
National String Instrument Corporation
United States (Los Angeles, California),
1934
Nickel alloy plated with nickel silver,
ebony, plastic
38⅝ × 14⅜ × 3⅜ in. (98 × 36.2 × 8.4 cm)
Museum of Fine Arts, Boston; Helen B.
Sweeney Fund 1998.193

PAGE 114 Resonator guitar (model 65
prototype)
Dobro Company
United States (Los Angeles, California),
1929
Magnolia, mahogany, ebony, aluminum
38 × 14¼ × 3¼ in. (96.4 × 36.2 × 8.2 cm)
Walter Carter

PAGE 116 Lap steel guitar (A-22 model)
Electro String Instrument Corporation
(Rickenbacker brand)
United States (Los Angeles, California),
1934
Cast aluminum
28⅝ × 7 × 1¾ in. (72.7 × 17.8 × 4.2 cm)
Stan Werbin, Elderly Instruments,
Lansing, Michigan

PAGE 119 Lap steel guitar (BD model)
Electro String Instrument Corporation
(Rickenbacker brand)
United States (Los Angeles, California),
about 1950
Plastic
29½ × 9¼ × 1¾ in. (74.9 × 23.5 × 4.4 cm)
Stan Werbin, Elderly Instruments, Lansing,
Michigan

PAGE 120 Lap steel guitar
(Dynamic model)
Valco (National brand)
United States (Chicago, Illinois), 1952
Wood, plastic
32 × 6½ × 1½ in. (81.3 × 16.5 × 3.8 cm)
Walter Carter

PAGE 121 Lap steel guitar
(Ultratone model)
Gibson, Inc.
United States (Kalamazoo, Michigan),
about 1949
Maple, plastic
32¾ × 8⅛ × 1⅞ in. (83 × 20.5 × 4.7 cm)
Walter Carter

PAGE 124 Electric guitar (Telecaster
model)
Fender Electric Instrument Company
United States (Fullerton, California), 1957
Ash, maple
38⅜ × 12⅝ × 1¾ in. (97.5 × 32 × 4.5 cm)
Brian Fischer

PAGE 126 Pair of electric guitars
(Stratocaster model)
Fender Electric Instrument Company
United States (Fullerton, California),
1963 and 1964
Ash, maple, rosewood
37⅞ × 12¼ × 1⅝ in. (96 × 31 × 4 cm)
Brian Fischer

PAGE 129 Electric guitar (Les Paul model)
Gibson, Inc.
United States (Kalamazoo, Michigan),
possibly late 1950s
Mahogany, ebony, mother-of-pearl, plastic
39 × 13 × 2 in. (99 × 33 × 5.1 cm)
Les Paul

PAGE 130 Electric guitar (Les Paul model)
Gibson, Inc.
United States (Kalamazoo, Michigan), 1952
Mahogany, maple, rosewood, mother-of-
pearl, plastic
39⅝ × 13 × 2 in. (100 × 33 × 5.1 cm)
Brian Fischer

PAGE 133 Electric guitar (Roundup
6130 model)
The Fred Gretsch Company, Inc.
United States (Brooklyn, New York), 1955
Mahogany, pine, rosewood, mother-of-
pearl, plastic, leather
39 × 13⅜ × 1⅞ in. (99 × 34 × 4.8 cm)
Scot Michael Arch

PAGE 135 Electric guitar (Flying V model)
Gibson, Inc.
United States (Kalamazoo, Michigan), 1958
Limba wood, rosewood
43⅜ × 16¾ × 1½ in. (110 × 42.5 × 3.8 cm)
Brian Fischer

PAGE 137 Electric guitar (Explorer model)
Gibson, Inc.
United States (Kalamazoo, Michigan), 1963
Limba wood, rosewood
43 × 17 × 1½ in. (109.2 × 43.1 × 3.8 cm)
Scot Michael Arch

PAGE 138 Electric guitar (White Falcon
6136 model)
The Fred Gretsch Company, Inc.
United States (Brooklyn, New York), 1956
Maple, spruce, ebony, mother-of-pearl,
plastic
42⅜ × 16⅞ × 2⅞ in.
(107.8 × 42.6 × 7.1 cm)
Mac Yasuda

PAGE 140 Electric guitar (6120 model)
The Fred Gretsch Company, Inc.
United States (Brooklyn, New York), 1955
Maple, rosewood, mother-of-pearl, plastic
41⅜ × 15⅝ × 2⅞ in.
(104.8 × 39.6 × 7.1 cm)
Chet Atkins

PAGE 141 Electric guitar (ES-335 model)
Gibson, Inc.
United States (Kalamazoo, Michigan), 1958
Maple, spruce, mahogany, rosewood,
plastic
41⅜ × 16⅛ × 1⅝ in. (105 × 41 × 4.1 cm)
Brian Fischer

PAGE 144 Electric guitar (Les Paul/
SG Standard model)
Gibson, Inc.
United States (Kalamazoo, Michigan), 1961
Mahogany, rosewood, mother-of-pearl,
plastic
39⅜ × 13 × 2⅞ in. (100 × 33 × 7.3 cm)
Brian Fischer

PAGE 145 Double-neck electric guitar
(EDS-1275 model)
Gibson, Inc.
United States (Kalamazoo, Michigan), 1960
Maple, spruce, rosewood, mother-of-pearl,
plastic
44 × 17¼ × 1⅞ in. (111.8 × 43.8 × 4.8 cm)
Courtesy of the Chinery Collection

PAGE 146 Electric guitar (360-12 model)
Electro String Instrument Corporation
(Rickenbacker brand)
United States (Los Angeles, California),
1966
Maple, padauk, plastic
39⅞ × 14⅞ × 1½ in. (101 × 37.5 × 3.8 cm)
Brian Fischer

PAGE 147 Electric guitar (Mk VI model)
Vox Company
England and Italy, late 1960s
Mahogany, ebony, plastic
41⅜ × 12⅜ × 1¾ in. (105 × 31.4 × 4.5 cm)
Brian Fischer

PAGE 149 Electric guitar (3012 model)
Danelectro Corporation
United States (Neptune City, New Jersey),
about 1960
Hardboard, pine, rosewood
38 × 13¼ × 1⅝ in. (96.5 × 33.5 × 4.3 cm)
Brian Fischer

PAGE 150 Electric guitar (Telecaster Pink
Paisley model)
Fender Musical Instruments
United States (Fullerton, California), 1969
Ash, maple, printed paper
38⅜ × 12⅝ × 1¾ in. (97.5 × 32 × 4.5 cm)
Collection of the Fender Museum of
Music and the Arts

PAGE 153 Electric guitar (Bianka model)
Hoyer Guitars
Germany (Tennenlohe), 1961
Maple, spruce, ebony, mother-of-pearl,
plastic
42 × 17⅞ × 3¾ in.
(106.6 × 45.4 × 9.6 cm)
Courtesy of the Chinery Collection

PAGE 157 Guitar (Romancer model)
Mastro Industries
Designed by Mario Maccaferri
(1900–1993)
United States (New York, New York),
about 1960
Plastic
34⅜ × 12¾ × 3½ in. (87.5 × 32.3 × 9 cm)
Brian Fischer

PAGE 158 Electric guitar (Glenwood
99 model)
Valco (National brand)
United States (Chicago, Illinois), 1963–64
Plastic, rosewood, mother-of-pearl
39⅜ × 14⅝ × 1⅞ in. (100 × 37.2 × 4.5 cm)
Stan Werbin, Elderly Instruments, Lansing,
Michigan

PAGE 160 Electric guitar (7000 4V model)
Oliviero Pigini and Company (EKO brand)
Italy (Recanati), early 1960s
Plastic, rosewood
40 × 13⅝ × 1⅜ in. (101.7 × 34.5 × 3.4 cm)
Brian Fischer

PAGE 161 Electric guitar (Karak model)
Wandré Pioli (born 1926)
Italy (Cavriago), about 1965
Plastic, wood, aluminum, rosewood
42⅜ × 16⅝ × 1¾ in.
(107.7 × 42.2 × 4.2 cm)
Michael Wright, The Different Strummer

PAGE 162 Electric guitar (Dan Armstrong model)
Ampeg Company
United States (Linden, New Jersey), 1969–70
Plastic, maple, rosewood
$38\frac{3}{8} \times 13 \times 1\frac{3}{8}$ in. (97.2 × 33 × 3.2 cm)
Michael Wright, The Different Strummer

PAGE 165 Electric guitar (Veleno Original model)
John Veleno (born 1934)
United States (St. Petersburg, Florida), 1974
Chrome-plated aluminum
$39\frac{1}{2} \times 13 \times 1\frac{1}{2}$ in. (100.3 × 33 × 3.8 cm)
Michael Wright, The Different Strummer

PAGE 167 Acoustic/electric guitar (Adamas model)
Ovation Instruments Division of Kaman Music Corp.
United States (New Hartford, Connecticut), 1981
Plastic, carbon fiber, birch, mahogany
$41\frac{3}{4} \times 15\frac{3}{4} \times 6\frac{3}{8}$ in. (106 × 40 × 16 cm)
Ovation Instruments Division of Kaman Music Corp.

PAGE 167 Electric guitar (Electraglide model)
Andrew Bond
Scotland (near Inverness), 1985
Carbon graphite
$40\frac{3}{8} \times 13\frac{3}{8} \times 1\frac{5}{8}$ in. (102.6 × 34 × 4.1 cm)
Michael Wright, The Different Strummer

PAGE 170 Electric guitar (331 model)
Electro String Instrument Company (Rickenbacker brand)
United States (Los Angeles, California), 1971
Maple, mahogany, plastic
$39\frac{3}{8} \times 14\frac{7}{8} \times 2$ in. (100 × 37.5 × 5.1 cm)
Brian Fischer

PAGE 171 Electric guitar (IC300 Artist Iceman)
Ibanez Company
Japan, 1978
Ash, maple, rosewood
$43 \times 14 \times 1\frac{1}{2}$ in. (109.2 × 35.5 × 3.8 cm)
Michael Wright, The Different Strummer

PAGE 172 Electric guitar (Flyte model)
Burns UK Ltd.
England (London), about 1976
Mahogany, maple, ebony
$40\frac{3}{4} \times 12\frac{1}{2} \times 1\frac{1}{2}$ in. (103.5 × 31.8 × 3.8 cm)
Michael Wright, The Different Strummer

PAGE 173 Electric guitar (M-1 model)
GRD
United States (South Strafford, Vermont), about 1978–80
Mahogany, rosewood, phenolic resin
$42\frac{7}{8} \times 11\frac{3}{8} \times 1\frac{7}{8}$ in. (108.7 × 28.8 × 4.8 cm)
Brian Fischer

PAGE 176 Electric guitar (2 × 4 model)
La Baye Company
United States (Green Bay, Wisconsin), 1967
Mahogany, rosewood, plastic
$44 \times 4\frac{1}{8} \times 2$ in. (111.8 × 10.5 × 5 cm)
Brian Fischer

PAGE 178 Electric guitar
Astron Engineering Enterprises
Alan Gittler (born 1928)
Israel, about 1987
Metal alloy
$28\frac{1}{2} \times 4\frac{1}{2} \times 1\frac{1}{4}$ in. (72.4 × 11.4 × 3.2 cm)
Michael Wright, The Different Strummer

PAGE 179 Electric guitar (GL2T model)
Steinberger Sound Company
United States (Newburgh, New York), 1986
Carbon graphite
$30\frac{1}{8} \times 7\frac{1}{2} \times 1\frac{7}{8}$ in. (76.5 × 19 × 4.5 cm)
Reeves Gabrels

PAGE 180 Travel guitar (customized Backpacker model)
Made by Robert McNally for the Martin Guitar Company
United States (Nazareth, Pennsylvania), 1994
Mahogany, spruce, ebony
$23 \times 6\frac{1}{2} \times 2$ in. (58.4 × 16.5 × 5.1 cm)
Courtesy of the Martin Guitar Company

PAGE 181 Chapman Stick
Stick Enterprises, Inc.
United States (Woodland Hills, California), 2000
Satine wood, paua shell
$43\frac{1}{2} \times 3\frac{1}{4} \times 1\frac{3}{4}$ in. (110.5 × 8.3 × 4.4 cm)
Museum of Fine Arts, Boston; Museum purchase with funds donated by Bradford M. and Dorothea R. Endicott 2000.581

PAGE 184 Electric guitar (M5-700 MoonSault model)
Kawai Company
Japan, 1982
Mahogany, rosewood, mother-of-pearl
$42 \times 12 \times 1\frac{5}{8}$ in. (106.7 × 30.5 × 4.1 cm)
Michael Wright, The Different Strummer

PAGE 185 Electric guitar (Pro II U series Urchin Deluxe model)
Arai Company (Aria trademark)
Japan, 1984
Ash, maple, rosewood
$40\frac{3}{4} \times 15 \times 1\frac{3}{4}$ in. (103.5 × 38.1 × 4.5 cm)
Michael Wright, The Different Strummer

PAGE 187 Electric guitar (Triaxe model)
Kramer (BKL) Company
United States (Neptune, New Jersey), 1986
Mahogany, rosewood
$35\frac{5}{8} \times 14\frac{5}{8} \times 1\frac{5}{8}$ in. (90.5 × 37.2 × 4.1 cm)
Michael Wright, The Different Strummer

PAGE 188 Digital guitar (DG1 model)
Stepp Ltd.
England (London), about 1987
Plastic
$41\frac{1}{2} \times 8\frac{3}{4} \times 2\frac{3}{8}$ in. (105.5 × 22 × 6 cm)
The Steve Howe Collection

PAGE 192 Electric guitar (Strawberry 6 custom model)
Mosrite Company
United States (Bakersfield, California), 1967
Maple, rosewood
$38 \times 9\frac{1}{2} \times 1\frac{3}{8}$ in. (96.5 × 24.1 × 3.2 cm)
Courtesy of the Chinery Collection

PAGE 194 Lap steel guitar
Semie Moseley (1935–1992)
United States (Jonas Ridge, North Carolina), 1984
Aluminum, rubber
$47\frac{1}{4} \times 8\frac{3}{8} \times 2\frac{3}{8}$ in. (120 × 21 × 5.8 cm)
America's Shrine to Music Museum, The University of South Dakota, Vermillion (No. 6190, Board of Trustees, 1998)

PAGE 195 Electric guitar (Yellow Cloud model)
David Rusan and Barry Haugen of Knut-Koupee Enterprises, Inc.
United States (Minneapolis, Minnesota), 1989
Maple
$39 \times 11 \times 2$ in. (99.1 × 27.9 × 5.1 cm)
National Museum of American History, Smithsonian Institution

PAGE 196 Electric guitar (five-neck custom model)
Hamer Guitars, Inc.
United States (Arlington Heights, Illinois), 1981
Mahogany, rosewood
$37\frac{7}{8} \times 29\frac{7}{8} \times 1\frac{7}{8}$ in. (96 × 76 × 4.5 cm)
Rick Nielsen

PAGE 198 Electric guitar (Les Paul custom model)
Gibson Guitar Corp. (Custom Division)
United States (Nashville, Tennessee), 1995
Mahogany, ebony, cocobolo, mother-of-pearl, abalone, plastic
$38\frac{7}{8} \times 13 \times 2$ in. (98.5 × 33 × 5.2 cm)
Kix Brooks

PAGE 201 Guitar (Pikasso model)
Linda Manzer (born 1952)
Canada (Toronto, Ontario), 1993
Rosewood, mahogany, spruce, ebony, abalone
$47 \times 18\frac{3}{8} \times 4$ in. (119.4 × 46.4 × 10.2 cm)
Courtesy of the Chinery Collection

PAGE 202 Coat-hanger electric guitar
Ken Butler (born 1948)
United States (Brooklyn, New York), 1991
Coat hangers, crutches, rulers, paper clips, bobby pins, guitar parts
$44 \times 14 \times 3$ in. (111.8 × 35.6 × 7.6 cm)
Ken Butler

PAGE 207 Electric guitar (Dragon 2000 model)
PRS Guitars
United States (Stevensville, Maryland), 1999
Maple, metal, shell, precious stone
$37\frac{5}{8} \times 13 \times 1\frac{1}{2}$ in. (95.5 × 33 × 3.8 cm)
PRS Guitars

PAGE 209 Electric guitar (Fly Artist model)
Parker Guitars
United States (Wilmington, Massachusetts), 1999
Spruce, carbon and glass fiber
$38 \times 12\frac{5}{8} \times 1\frac{5}{8}$ in. (96.5 × 32 × 4 cm)
Museum of Fine Arts, Boston; Gift of Parker Guitars 1999.739

PAGE 211 Acoustic/electric guitar (Chet Atkins SC model)
Gibson Guitars
United States (Nashville, Tennessee), 1993
Mahogany, spruce, ebony, abalone
$39\frac{3}{8} \times 14\frac{1}{2} \times 1\frac{7}{8}$ in. (100 × 36.8 × 4.6 cm)
Chet Atkins

PAGE 212 Prototype guitar (Opus 103)
William "Grit" Laskin (born 1953)
Canada (Toronto, Ontario), 1989
Rosewood, maple, spruce, ebony
$40 \times 14\frac{5}{8} \times 6\frac{1}{2}$ in. (101.5 × 37 × 16.5 cm)
Canadian Museum of Civilization

PAGE 215 Acoustic/electric guitar (Chrysalis model)
Chrysalis Guitar Co., Inc.
United States (New Boston, New Hampshire), 1999
Carbon graphite, Mylar, cloth
$39\frac{7}{8} \times 15\frac{1}{4} \times 1\frac{1}{4}$ in. (101 × 38.5 × 3 cm)
Tim White, Chrysalis Guitar Co., Inc.

PAGE 216 Arch-top guitar (Centura model)
James D'Aquisto (1935–1995)
United States (Greenport, New York), 1995
Maple, spruce, ebony
$43 \times 17 \times 3$ in. (109.2 × 43.2 × 7.6 cm)
Perry Beekman

FOR FURTHER READING

Bacon, Tony and Paul Day. *The Ultimate Guitar Book.* New York: Alfred A. Knopf, 1991.

Bacon, Tony and Scott Chinery. *The Chinery Collection: 150 Years of American Guitars.* London: Balafon Books, 1996.

Carter, Walter. *Gibson Guitars: 100 Years of an American Icon.* Los Angeles: General Publishing Group, 1994.

Evans, Tom and Mary Anne. *Guitars: Music, History, Construction and Players from the Renaissance to Rock.* New York: Facts on File, 1977.

Gruhn, George and Walter Carter. *Acoustic Guitars and Other Fretted Instruments: A Photographic History.* San Francisco: GPI Books/Miller Freeman, 1993.

Gruhn, George and Walter Carter. *Electric Guitars and Basses: A Photographic History.* San Francisco: GPI Books/Miller Freeman, 1994.

The Metropolitan Museum of Art. *The Spanish Guitar.* New York: The Metropolitan Museum of Art, 1992.

Romanillos, José L. *Antonio de Torres, Guitar Maker: His Life and Work.* Westport, CT: The Bold Strummer, 1987.

Smith, Richard R. *The Complete History of Rickenbacker Guitars.* Fullerton, CA: Centerstream Publishing, 1987.

Smith, Richard R. *Fender: The Sound Heard 'Round the World.* Fullerton, CA: Garfish Publishing Company, 1995.

Trynka, Paul. *The Electric Guitar: An Illustrated History.* San Francisco: Chronicle Books, 1995.

Tyler, James. *The Early Guitar.* London: Oxford University Press, 1980.

Washburn, Jim and Richard Johnston. *Martin Guitars: An Illustrated Celebration of America's Premier Guitarmaker.* Emmaus, PA: Rodale Press, 1997.

Wheeler, Tom. *American Guitars: An Illustrated History* (revised and updated edition). New York: Harper Perennial, 1992.

Wright, Michael. *Guitar Stories, Vol. 1: The Histories of Cool Guitars.* Bismarck, ND: Vintage Guitar Books, 1995.

Wright, Michael. *Guitar Stories, Vol. 2: The Histories of Cool Guitars.* Bismarck, ND: Vintage Guitar Books, 2000.